BIRD DOGS
AND
BETTY CAKES

To George Marcos:

It hopes that this book
Stirs memories of your own
Betty Cake-sweet
outdoors experiences.

Tom Carn

Also by Tom Carney:

Sun-Drenched Days, Two-Blanket Nights: A Sportsman Takes Note

Natural Wonders of Michigan: A Guide to Parks, Preserves & Wild Places

BIRD DOGS
AND
BETTY CAKES
More Notes from the Outdoors

Tom Carney

drawings by Glenn Wolff

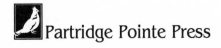
Partridge Pointe Press

The essays in this book first appeared, in slightly different form, in the *Oakland Press*, Pontiac, Michigan.

Cover design: Gail Dennis
Cover art: Glenn Wolff

ISBN 0-9637085-3-8

Printed in the United States of America.

5 4 3 2 1

for Maureen,
who through it all still finds the strength to call me, "Honey."
Usually.

Contents

Introduction

The inspiration for this book comes from the kindness of two sets of people.

First, dozens of readers of my first book, *Sun-Drenched Days, Two-Blanket Nights*, encouraged me by asking for more of the same. And in *Bird Dogs and Betty Cakes*, you will find similarities: a collection of essays—some serious, others allegedly humorous—arranged in chronological order.

Also, the pieces offer a smorgasbord of topics, all of which are based on outdoors activities or experiences with nature. Plus, they emphasize the special treats that await us if we take time to observe and appreciate.

For me the treats are as varied as the unbridled joy of watching a purebred dog doing what every gene in its body is programmed to do and the dizzyingly sweet dessert provided by a friend's loving wife—the recipe for which, by the way, you'll see follows this introduction, ready for photocopying.

The treats involve the calm instilled by a small pond as it rocks a solo canoe before daybreak, the successful corruption of a hard-working neighbor, the haunting song of a hermit thrush in the morning, the way that Maureen always seems to win.

Make no mistake, she does always come out on top and that is another similarity.

What's different is that this time, while assembling the essays I noticed certain themes and thoughts and influences make more than a single appearance. In that way, this book might suggest more unity than the first.

Also, I hope you find it's written better.

The second group of people responsible here are those who have allowed me what few writers get: the freedom to pack up my writing and head in whatever directions I choose—and on a regular basis, no less.

Since this book represents selections from my weekly newspaper column, you should realize the degree to which I enjoy the latitude to experiment and to just plain mess around when I write that column. Such freedom comes only through the benevolent indulgence of the folks in charge at the *Oakland Press*, especially Editor Neil J. Munro and Managing Editor Garry J. Gilbert.

If you enjoy reading the pieces as much as I enjoy producing them, I hope you will join me in offering thanks to these gentlemen.

Finally, thankfully, a third group aided in the presentation of the final product. Having seen all the mistakes I allowed to slip through my own judicious editing, I am sure you will join me in thanking Norris McDowell, Eldon Thomas and Maureen herself, for volunteering to review the copy.

Tom Carney
December 1997

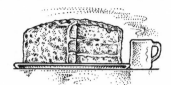

Betty Cake

INGREDIENTS:
1 box yellow or white cake mix w/pudding
2 1/2 cups sugar
1 cup whole milk

1/2 stick butter
1/2 cup water
3 mashed, over-ripe bananas
(or more if desired)

3 eight-inch cake pans

DIRECTIONS:
Bake cake mix according to directions on box. While it is baking, mix the milk, butter and 2 cups of sugar. Cook until it becomes a thick syrup.

Mix the bananas into 1/2 cup sugar and the water. Cook for a few minutes then add to the syrup. The consistency should be fairly thick with chunks of bananas.

After the cake has completely cooled, punch holes in each layer, one at a time. Pour the banana syrup onto the cake, letting it drain into the cake through the holes. Use more syrup as an icing for the layer. Repeat this process with the remaining two layers. If any syrup remains, glaze the entire cake.

Somebody Loves Lucy

SEPTEMBER 1992

I really hadn't considered the possibility until the night before the breeder delivered her to our cabin last month. The Sandman wrestled unsuccessfully with my excitement and I began chattering and "what-iffing." Maureen set down her magazine and raised the question.

"What if the puppy turns out to be orange-ticked instead of black?"

"I hardly consider that a possibility, my dear," I graciously implied as I rolled towards her and shouted, "What are you, nuts? She's Paddy's niece's daughter so she'll have black ticks."

"OK, Tom. Whatever you say. I just don't want you to be disappointed. So, what are we going to name her?"

Maureen was still holding out for "Molly," but our friends had beaten us by a week with their new puppy and had used it. Try again.

"But you guys never bird hunt together," she said. "The dogs will never be together. They'll never know."

"You just don't name your dog the same as your friend's dog. Not if it's still alive anyway."

Guy ethics, I told her, bound us to continue the nomination process and I came up with a suggestion of my own: "How about 'Goo-goo'?"

"No way!" Maureen herself graciously implied with a finger flick to my forehead and said, "Goo-goo this!"

The next night, the conversation continued with increased intensity and necessity while Puppy was in her cage sleeping away.

"She's got orange ticks, Mo."

"Yeah. So what?"

"I wanted a dog with black ticks. Plus there's no patch over her eye. And I wanted a dog with a patch. But you know what's the worst?"

"I'm afraid to ask," she replied.

"She's got a pink nose. I hate dogs with pink noses."

"You know what, Tom?"

"What's that?"

"I think she's just adorable. And she's the dog you have. So you'll just have to get used to her."

"Yeah, yeah," I said. "So what do you want to call her? With that red nose and ears, she can be 'Bozo.' What does that do for you?"

It made her want to give me another finger flick, then another when I suggested "Baloney Nose."

All that name deciding gave me a headache. So I left the choice up to Maureen, and now we have a little "Lucy" who's learning from Maggie how to jump onto the couch and practice restin'. However, she still needs to be lifted onto the bed in the middle of the night so Maggie can teach her how to snuggle.

Lucy is an orange belton, or ticked, English setter; Maggie, a black. While fully grown Maggie is light at 33 pounds, Lucy the puppy is already 23 pounds. She's a bundle of joy, love and energy. In the last month, she's renovated my heart. Where I thought it only contained room to love one dog—that being Paddy who died last year—she's expanded its square footage adding an entirely new Lucy wing. She's my first dog in 20 years who gives kisses. Her energy is boundless; she's always ready to mess around. And unlike most little females, she's never left a puddle indoors from an exhibition of submissiveness.

"Wouldn't it be neat," I suggested to Maureen the morning after we named the puppy, "if Lucy ended up with Paddy's hunting intensity and Maggie's personality."

"She'd be a perfect dog," said Maureen.

So far, however, Lucy's exhibited Paddy's personality. She's bold, inquisitive and headstrong to a certain degree. And she's begun teaching Maggie the little lady a few bad habits, like how to dig. At home, Lucy's favorite excavation site is alongside the deck which she will then crawl beneath and get stuck under. One time she whimpered there until Maureen found her and dug her out. No sooner had Maureen set Lucy down and turned to fill in the cavity than Lucy's little white bucket butt with the big orange spot stared back from beneath the deck.

As a hunting dog, Lucy shoulders the burden of my dreams for the next decade of Octobers. So I took her to the woods opening weekend with mixed emotions: hope for Lucy, lingering sadness over the loss of Paddy and uncertainty over my own ability and desire to locate birds without him streaking ahead of me. After four hours of hunting, however, I had only managed to locate four birds for Lucy. She hadn't seen them, though, and I missed the only woodcock at which I had shot. For some reason, perhaps fueled by my own sense of inadequacy, perhaps by my need to prove once and for all that without Paddy my hunting would be nothing more than a charade, I led Lucy to the spot of the once-great woodcock hunt.

Perhaps we both were led, for during our hour-long foray we flushed nine woodcock. Luck donated three birds to my game bag. But the last two shots must have required some degree of skill on my part, for tears blurred my view. You see, the very first bird would have been lost if not for Lucy.

She watched it launch into the air and begin its flight. She watched it fall, with my shot, through the aspen crowns into the thick grass below. Like a puppy— all ears and bounce and butt — she galloped to the area to investigate.

In one of those clarifying mystic moments on whose wings insight arrives, she stopped, reconsidered, then like a well-trained dog picked up the bird and delivered it to me. Her first retrieve on the first bird we had taken together.

As I knelt to accept her offering, tears over the loss of Paddy blended with those over Lucy's performance at the tender age of

three and a half months. Best of all, they were licked away by the
first dog in 20 years who gives me kisses.

And now I have the utmost of hope for the little girl dog. Even for
her nose. Why just this afternoon she came in from playing and I
noticed a line, an encroaching dark color—yes, it's black—starting
at the back of her nose. The tint must be creeping forward! Yes!

"That's just dirt from her garden excavation, you goof," Maureen
suggested subtly.

Actually, the finger flick communicated the message just fine all
by itself.

Kindling Spirits

They still throw some light and some heat. And they remain welcome, nearly essential components of a fine outdoors experience. But something has changed about my fires lately.

If it's correct to say that life evolved from the sea, is it equally correct to suggest that fire burst open the cone to release the seeds of our humanity? In other words, if saline water provides the basis of protoplasm, living tissue and body chemistry, what about flames? After all, for us fires seem to spark story telling, mystic musings and cogitation. Why presume a different effect on ancient man? Is it accurate, therefore, to say that fire inspired literature and drama, religion, science and technology?

Like eternal moths, we're drawn to flames. Perhaps we identify with fire's basic contradictions: it's a great destroyer while at the same time it provides for new growth; it's beautiful yet dangerous; the more it seems brilliantly alive, the closer it moves toward extinguishment; it is an important tool for survival as well as enthralling entertainment; a torch, it illuminates other things, yet remains a welcoming chamber in which to lose oneself.

Until about a year ago, with such thoughts I'd lose myself in *camp fires*. Now they are simply *fires*.

And they crinkle now where once they cracked and spat.

For the last several years, we enjoyed our piece of northern Michigan from the warmth and comfort of an old Air Stream-type trailer my brother-in-law Bruce had graciously donated to the cause. While it had a perfectly functional propane heater, more often than not— after we opened up and unpacked the truck—our chief order of business was to get a camp fire going.

We had scraped out a fire pit 20 feet from the trailer, just about where the wood burning stove would sit if we could get that cabin built. Hot summer or cold autumn nights made no difference; the only variable was how closely to the fire we'd pull our lawn chairs during the cribbage games.

Once, a forester for the Michigan Department of Natural Resources came out to help me figure out what trees to cut for firewood.

Hardwood, he said, like oak, maple, beech and ash, is excellent for "important" fires, those used for heating and cooking. These are the fires whose flames burn low, slowly and whose lazy embers might be coaxed into staying around 'til morning. On the other hand, softwood like pine, cedar, fir and aspen, is OK to use for "recreational" fires. These intense but short-lived blazes will set the mood yet die down by bedtime.

Surprisingly, all wood gives off the same amount of heat, he told us. For example, a pound of aspen will produce as much heat as a pound of oak. It just takes more aspen to make a pound.

Then, so even I could understand, he explained the point more simply: oak is more dense, so an armload of it will weigh more than an armload of aspen. As a result, it will throw off more heat than the armload of aspen.

That was helpful to know, but most of the time we were shooting for atmosphere, not heat. Good thing, for aspen, jack pine and cedar are the most abundant types available throughout the property.

So, starting with the brush piles closest to the campsite, I'd gather tinder and kindling, break intermediate size wood and drag over some logs. A few armloads in the afternoon prepared us, and massive, quick burning blazes became the order of the night. The cedar would crack and pop, the pine's sap would sizzle and the aspen would get the burning over in a spirited yet business-like manner. Sometimes, from our beds in the trailer we could see the light from the flames timidly wading into the darkness beyond the clearing.

Camp fires have become fires because now we have a cabin with a fireplace. Now we can sit comfortably protected against the elements and tell stories, muse mystically or cogitate.

Since we rely on the fireplace to heat the cabin, our woodpile consists mostly of oak, maple and beech, the stuff that burns low and slow. Scrub kindling has been replaced by Georgia fatwood from a mail order catalogue. Also, a few trips from woodpile to cabin with an armload of logs, common sense and my weak back convinced me to order a wood hauling cart while I was at it.

From the cart I've drawn a couple starter logs; from the kindling bucket, three pieces of fatwood. Some newspaper, a match and a fireplace with a good draft complete the tools needed to heat things up.

On this frigid morning, dawn hesitates in her approach. The coffee maker has sputtered a deposit in my cup. The dogs have come back in, preferring the comfort of their couch to the lyrical snow that has begun to fall.

I close the book I have been reading and shut off the lamp. All is darkness except for the reassuring glow from the calm fire. All is quiet except for the soothing crinkle of those logs as they surrender themselves to the irresistible advances of heat and oxygen. All is still, save for the pulsing of the flames.

The puppy murmurs in her sleep as the fire cradles us in our contentment.

For now, anyway, I don't miss camp fires.

Field Maneuvers

AUGUST 1993

O ne feature found in many American homes is the "honey-do" jar. Often nothing more elaborate than a coffee can decorated with wrapping paper, the jar acts as a repository for all those little reminders, written in feminine handwriting, and all composed in the same basic format: "Honey, will you please ... " do this or that?

Experienced honeys realize that the question is a mere formality, the *please* a mere nod in the direction of manners. They know a decree when they hear one. Master honeys develop the uncanny ability to convince the honey masters that the optimum time to attend to the tasks is during the lull in major outdoor activities which occurs between last ice and the opening of trout season. The neophytes and apprentices among us must try our luck with less conventional approaches.

I have been able to forestall installation of this note-propagating appliance by convincing Maureen that I must attend to "projects." Besides, Maureen knows we march to the paces of different drum- mers; thus it does her no good to pressure me to take on tasks which she has proven time and again she is more than capable of complet- ing herself—and on her own schedule.

For example, in the nine short years we've been married, she's taught herself to mow and fertilize the lawn, prepare walls and windows for painting, replace a toilet, fish electrical wires to boxes and outlets and recently, to tune the eight-cylinder engine on the Suburban. In that time, I've been consumed with my workroom peg board installation and tool hanging project. This was immediately followed by the hanging tool outline tracing with a felt marker project, one which snatches so much attention because it must be done right the first time. Plus it demands no small degree of artistic focus.

With that concern just about wrapped up, I have recently enjoyed the pleasure of moving beyond the one room in the basement. In fact, I've even embarked upon a couple of yard projects. All the while, Maureen does her best to hide her appreciation of my efforts. She'll pretend that she actually wants me to help with the trifles upon which she idles away her time. Kind of like what happened a few weeks ago:

"Tom!" Maureen called from the bedroom she was remodeling. "For the last time, would you please come inside and help me finish tearing out this drywall?"

"Can't!" I answered from the backyard. "I'm in the middle of a ground scan, waste retrieval and disposal project."

As she rushed outside to take a prideful look at my work she said, "You can leave those apples on the lawn with the others that have been there all summer. I need you to—Oww! Oh man! Doggone it, Lucy!"

"What's the matter?" I asked. "Look how you scared Lucy," our setter who had turned tail and dashed behind the shed.

"Oh, I twisted my ankle in another one of the holes she's dug"

"Those aren't holes," I offered. "That's her soil redistribution project."

Once again Maureen deftly concealed her appreciation: "Just empty that garbage can and—"

"You mean the S.P.C.V."

"What?"

"The Sector Patrol Command Vehicle," I informed her.

"Whatever. Just get that garbage bag out of there and—"

"That would be the P.C.P.," I politely corrected.

"I'm afraid to ask. What's that?"

"The Payload Containment Pouch."

"Never mind," she said, spinning back toward the house and creating a husband relocation project of her own in the process.

I've had more than my share of projects at the cabin in the year that we've owned it, too.

My wood duck housing project attracted 15 eggs but no hatchlings. My firewood economizing project left me with a sore back and too many more logs to cut down to size. And my personal weight reduction project fell flat when I discovered a half gallon of ice cream and a quart of blueberries our guests had left behind in the freezer.

The most ambitious and long-range project to date has been my piscatorial habitat improvement project. It began after the first of the year with my hauling our Christmas tree onto the ice near our dock. By Easter the tree had partially sunk. By the end of April, it had floated back to shore halfway to our neighbor's cabin.

Finally, with a piece of cinder block, I weighted it down, closer to our dock, just within fly casting range so I could enjoy the bluegill and crappie it would surely entice.

I don't know how long these projects take to mature: a year, maybe two? So I've saved that spot all summer, paddling carefully by it and casting my line expertly and respectfully around but not close to it.

Last weekend, while I sat on the dock dreaming of the day I'd haul some big bluegill from my spot, a slow moving shadow drew my attention. Too vain to wear glasses, I squinted against both the reflection and my dreary eyesight. Wow! A nice, big pike patrolled the area and encouraged me to rush to the cabin for a rod with a big lure. He allowed only one cast to interrupt his cruising, though. In an instant, he was hooked and fighting against the pressure the rod and I applied. In another instant, he worked free, the lure whizzing past my head.

"Maureen! Come down here! Quick!" I called while casting again.

"What happened? Are you all right?" she asked, scurrying down the ladder and in her haste nearly losing her hammer and scattering what remained of the square of shingles.

"Man oh man!" I sputtered. "I just lost a big pike."

"That's all? I nearly fell off the roof for this news flash?"

"But it was really neat. You should have seen him before he got away."

"Ohhh, I get it," she nodded, giving me the same look I've seen when I extol the athletic skills exhibited by synchronized swimmers. "You must have enrolled him in your project for icthyological deception, education and premature reintroduction to the environment."

"I did?" I asked. "Oh yeah. Something like that."

"Now it's time for Phase I of the house commander tension relieving project," she said ushering me up the ladder with the claw of the hammer.

From the lounge chair in the shade she further instructed, "For Phase II, you head to the florist. And be sure to take along a credit card."

Time Out in Time

AUGUST 1993

What constitutes a *classic*? And at what point do you feel its embrace?

Years ago, like any wholesome American college student, I never felt the embrace of any of the assigned classics. Instead, they would seize my attention in a choke hold for the two class sessions during which they'd be discussed, plus the quizzes. No love lost there.

And while he favored athletes, John Rowe Workman, my classics professor at Brown University, was far from amused when I opined, "A literary classic is something they developed before they had the technology to produce sleeping pills. No lie."

(Survival tip for students: *No lie* at the end of a statement is not a viable substitute for a footnote in your college research papers.)

After nearly two decades of periodic revisits to *The Odyssey*, though, I've learned to appreciate its most important quality, the one prominent in every definition of the term *classic*: the durability of its message and the timelessness of its appeal.

Recently, I enjoyed a classic night on the pond.

Something made me turn from the petite, graceful, five-foot long graphite spinning rod I always use. Instead, I resurrected the Fenwick, fiberglass and six inches longer. It was the first high quality piece of fishing gear I ever afforded myself, back in 1973. It's also been neglected for the better part of a decade.

There's nothing wrong with the Fenwick. Just that it has been relegated to second-string status and, like a coach with a blowout on his mind, I had never substituted. In fact, I once gave the rod to Maureen, although now I remind her I had only loaned it.

Fishing with the Fenwick also means employing its partner, the Quick 110N reel. It's at least twice as big as the tiny reel for the graphite rod and its cast metal body from West Germany easily makes it twice as heavy. Tough to believe but twenty years earlier the Fenwick and the Quick passed for "ultra-lite" gear.

Running the line through the guides of the rod and reacquainting myself with its cork grip, I sensed, I think, the same eager anticipation with which Odysseus strings his bow after his twenty-year absence. With the reel and rod adjusted to a balance which suited me and with my eye on the awaiting water, I sensed a confidence much like Odysseus does, I'm sure, when he nocks the arrow to shoot through the ax heads.

As far as clothing, instead of expensive sneakers or boots, I slipped into my old pair of deck shoes. These shoes have stepped past "well worn" and beyond the threshold of "insult inviting." Their white rubber soles have yellowed with time. Miles have eroded the ridges on those soles into slick plains.

The leather uppers of the shoes have aged individually. Above the toes and along the outer edge of the left shoe, about half the stitching has simply vanished like one's youth, and the tongue wags freely on that side. The leather on the inner edge of the right shoe has worn from the sole, probably encouraged by the callus that distorts my big toe—a reminder of the motorboat clunking that befell me in the Bahamas.

When pressed into action, these shoes are a walking contradiction: not worth the cost of repair, too valuable to toss away.

To deflect the approaching chill, I donned my green 60/40 parka, the one I had bought for backpacking in the Smoky Mountains in 1974. The 60/40 indicated the material that we used before the arrival of Gore-Tex. It never totally discouraged water but was the best you could do. Throughout the seasons, stress on the left pocket has ripped the sutures I had placed to repair a four-inch gash. And once when I tried to untangle stubborn fishing line, I snagged just enough of it near my wrist to remind me that my next jacket must not have Velcro on the cuffs.

Only one hat could suitably cap off this selection of gear. Rummaging through the hat shelf, I poked past the others, the camouflage and the neon green. I brushed aside the Stetson which I reserve for ear protection when I'm fly fishing. No, only one hat would do: a white nylon baseball cap whose patch sports a yellow border and green lettering which reads "Johnson Reels."

To be accurate, you should say the cap is "once-white." It's so filthy that Maureen has graciously excused either it or herself from every photograph since the first fishing trip after our wedding. The foam has disintegrated beneath the mesh of both the once-white forehead band and the green underside of the visor. There used to be a tag inside, just an American flag and "Made in the U.S.A." Some of the cap's piping hangs in tatters. It's a cap people would expect to see about six feet above those deck shoes.

Thus outfitted, like Odysseus disguised as a beggar, I paddled away in my solo canoe which, as my preferred vessel for these waters, has become a classic in its own right.

Long about prime fishing time, falling temps suggested I zip up the parka. More and more flies began fluttering above and settling upon the pond. The surface kisses of the smaller bluegill became slurps of larger ones. And accompanying the kisses and slurps were the calm body rolls of bigger fish feeding with easy confidence, assured by the knowledge that there would be plenty for all.

A fair-sized smallmouth bass gave my Fenwick and me a little fun. As I was releasing him, the tremolo of a loon conferred on us a blessing from just beyond the southern edge of the pond. A beaver moseying downstream nonchalantly glanced my way and, once recognition set in, immediately tail-slapped itself into temporary exile beneath the surface.

I quit fishing, sat back and succumbed to nature as a light breeze wafted the canoe homeward.

Now in a corner of the porch at our cabin, the Fenwick and the Quick stand ever alert and ready for action. On a hook near the door the once-white cap hangs above the green jacket. The restless shoes await below.

Professor Workman would be impressed, I'm sure, for I have clearly defended my thesis. Classics, indeed, can inspire sweet dreams.

No lie.

Priorities

What a difference a year makes.

Before bird season last year, I was filled with anticipation, anxiety, worry.

This year, I'm filled with worry, anticipation, anxiety.

All because of a dog.

Although she had no idea, last year at this time Lucy, our new English setter puppy, was getting ready for her first hunting season. I had to tell myself that I shouldn't expect too much, that 1992 would be her "fun" year. That the most I could hope for would be her learning to love being outdoors with me and that just maybe, with a little luck, she'd stumble onto a bird or two by season's end. And of course, I agonized over the possibility that my dreams of countless golden autumn days afield with her would be dashed because she might prove to be weak at hunting, or worse, uninterested.

This year, my only worry is that I'll be the one to mess things up.

That's because last year, things went much more smoothly than anticipated. By the middle of August, Lucy was ranging in front of me through some rye fields—just enough foliage to get her used to it. And I had successfully acclimated her to the discharge of a .410 shotgun.

Through Sunday morning of opening weekend, at only three and a half months old, Lucy had convinced me that at best my dreams would have to be put on hold for a year. Sunday afternoon, however, she convinced me to dream on and to a greater degree.

She retrieved three woodcock that afternoon. Ten days later, still not four months old, she pointed her first birds. For the rest of the season, I didn't shoot at a woodcock unless she pointed it. Even so, I ended up with the chance to take more than in any previous season.

In October she made a multiple blind retrieve—locating two birds that had fallen in two separate spots in thick cover— an achievement that often distinguishes winners from losers in retriever trials. By November she handled three grouse like a pro. When we hung up her hunting collar after her first season, she was little more than five months old.

She is on the road to becoming a good dog.

If I don't mess up.

I've told myself I won't press her too hard. I won't get frustrated and try to teach her too much at one time. I won't lose my temper when training. In short, I'm trying to avoid all the mistakes I made with my first dog.

The two biggest mistakes I made and am currently struggling against are comparing Lucy to other dogs and gauging how much she needs to be trained as opposed to standing back and letting her abilities take over.

Another mistake I should guard against is forgetting that she still is involved in her education. It will be a real challenge to me to remember that she might make mistakes this fall, that my efforts in training have only just begun. I must also guard against a tendency to over-handle her in the field.

Part of the reason we over-handle dogs, I believe, is in an effort to show our hunting buddies how much control we have over the pup. Well, that ends up being a prime indicator of another major mistake we tend to make: bragging unduly about our dogs. Too much bragging puts unnecessary stress on both the dog and the hunter. For in order to save face, the more the hunter has bragged, the more he needs to be sure the dog performs "properly." Hence, the over-handling.

Every gene in that little dog's body is programmed to sniff, stalk and point birds; I must be careful not to interfere. For if I succumb to the urge to correct, discipline or even punish her too much, whose deficiencies am I showcasing? If I over-handle her for fear of negative critiques about her performance from my hunting partners, what's that saying about my dedication to the team she and I are trying to form? Moreover, what does that say about the quality of human companions with whom I've chosen to step afield?

My ulcers start to percolate, my pulse increases, my stomach performs gymnastics from such self-induced worry. Then my mind steps in with some gentle reminders: Lucy trying to scale the lilac bush in the back yard in an effort to get closer to birds; Lucy racing to the basement and pasting herself to my side when, upon rummaging through the gunning bag for my compass, I inadvertently jingle her hunting bell; Lucy transformed from a dispassionate dozer to a dervish of desire when the hunting video's narrator mentions the magic word "birds"; Lucy riding impassively in the cage all the while we drive on blacktop but whimpering to be released the moment we sneak onto dirt roads and she sees bird cover; Lucy, a week before she turned four months old, gliding onto point just like a big dog because for some reason she knew that was the right thing to do; Lucy, a month later, little chubby butt wobbling on hind legs, trying to secure a woodcock I had shot by straight-arming the trunk of the small aspen tree which had snagged it.

Images like these are a reminder that for many of us, bird hunting is not our passion; hunting with good bird dogs is.

With that thought planted foremost in our minds, we can settle down and allow most other concerns to jostle among themselves for a distant second place.

Bird Dogs and Betty Cakes

OCTOBER 1993

With traditional scenes, props and even memorized lines, our hunting camp takes on the guise of some grand theater production with a limited engagement in the Upper Peninsula's woods each October. And a tossed salad of pals provides enough personalities to assume roles as needed.

Jim Ekdahl, a conservation officer from Baraga, sent each of us a tantalizing warm-up a few weeks before this year's confluence in the woods. The story he had found mentioned the four stereotypical roles hunters end up playing in some aboriginal tribes. He wondered whether our camp's personalities shake out in the same manner.

Certainly the first role, that of huntmaster or leader, falls on camp founder Tom Huggler. It was he who began the social experiment of inviting several friends to join him in an annual foray after grouse and woodcock; it was he who introduced most of them to the joys of hunting behind fine pointing dogs; it is he who, near the middle of each August, sends the "only about six weeks until camp" letter, the equivalent of "Gentlemen, start your engines."

And there is no dearth of candidates to share the second role, the trickster/fool, on a daily basis, some permanent. And if one of us is lucky in a particular year, he might be able to assume the elusive mantle of spearman/tracker, the expert hunter.

"And I nominate Norris for shaman," the final role, Ekdahl's note concluded.

Norris McDowell discharges the duties of camp high priest and visionary as if the role were written with him in mind. It is Norris, more than anyone, whose sheer, unabashed joy over being in camp transcends words. His five-day perpetual smile alone is evidence that he's living the dream he envisions the remaining 360 days of the year. And like a shaman, Norris immerses himself in the camp rituals such as reading from the Holy Writ—fine outdoor literature—as we sit around the campfire.

Norris exudes the essence of camp, true, but his wife Betty has become indispensable. At least if you ask me she has. At least her handiwork has. Because I always pretend that she bakes just for me a special cake that I covet and sometimes hide from the others. And after what happened this year, Norris has threatened to hide it from me.

After pitching his tent and while he, Dick Bradley and I awaited the arrival of the full complement of campers for opening night, Norris dispensed me to his cooler to fetch us each a beer. I returned with two beers and a silly grin.

"Carney, you didn't," Norris pleaded, though he knows me too well to expect otherwise.

I simply revealed what remained of the glob of Betty cake I had taken the liberty to snatch then simply reveled in its sinful sweetness.

"You dog," he continued. "That's supposed to be for everybody."

"Not my fault they're late," I replied, licking my fingers with absolutely no remorse. And then, "You guys need another beer yet?"

Betty makes this wonderful cake, so rich and sweet that it honestly made me swoon the first time it danced upon my tongue. My knees buckled. No lie. The recipe, passed down by her Aunt Susie, calls for a white cake with a banana flavored glaze. It doesn't look like anything special but the cake is so sweet, moist and tasty that we developed a phrase for anything superfluous or excessive: "That's like putting icing on a Betty cake."

This year, she sent along a second, equally scrumptious product from her oven, and we've altered our saying to reflect the plural.

On the first full day of camp, Thursday, a hailstorm ambushed Ekdahl, Ron Barger, my setter Lucy and me about a mile from the

Suburban. When we finally reached it, Lucy dove beneath the truck in a full lay-out position. The rest of us hopped around trying to figure out who had the keys, the tiny ice balls giggling as they tiptoed down the backs of our necks. Washed out, we sought a place to dry our clothes.

South Republic is smaller than a one-traffic light town. The single traffic light there, we were told, works only the afternoon shift with a little overtime. No traffic to speak of during the day or after the bars close.

In South Republic, we found a Laundromat/bait shop. Honest to goodness that's what the place was. We sat there in the spare clothes we had thoughtfully brought along as our blaze orange jackets and vests tumbled in the dryers along with our pants and socks.

Now, instead of a traditional baseball cap, Barger prefers a remnant from his days spent further south. It's one of those long-billed caps that fishermen wear in the Florida Keys. As we waited, he surveyed the scene. Then his eyes indicated company. Jim and I turned to look.

In strolls this character who belongs in anyone's repertoire. In the otherwise empty building, he sizes us up from a distance, apparently discerns we are bird hunters, approaches our group and begins to make some bird hunter small talk.

From beneath his filthy Atlanta Braves cap sprouts a pair of items which resemble Elvis sideburns dipped in RapidGro. Just off-center along his upper gum, a single tooth holds on for dear life. It must turn in yeoman's work, for the filthy, tattered, plaid flannel shirt strains where it circles his belly. A tobacco tin has left its mark in the pocket. His blue jeans, of course, are likewise filthy and torn. And it's obvious he's done everything except run in his Nike jogging shoes which I'm pretty sure were once white. If he had a pierced ear, he could have been a grunge rocker.

"Lemme' tell you boys sumpin'," he says in a dialect that sounds more like southern Ohio than Upper Peninsula. Before continuing, he takes a furtive glance over each shoulder. Barger calls this the "cartoon stealth take."

Then, with what Ekdahl calls the "conspiratorial step-in," he moves one stride closer to our group and shares his illicit secret: "On openin' day, I got me 17 pats."

Pats means *grouse* and the limit is five per day. And all his conspiratorial step-in achieves is to move him one stride closer to a conservation officer, in whose presence his cartoon stealth take had assured him he was not. We all just nod, acting not at all impressed.

"I could probably guide ya' there."

"What about woodcock?" asks Barger.

"Who cares about them?" our visitor says. "They're too hard to hit."

We remain silent, still unimpressed. So he applies gas to the flames, allowing as how he does enjoy the sport of shooting woodcock as they fly in at dusk. He's also admitting to another game violation, by the way.

Barger can stand it no longer. From deep beneath that long visor he goads the guy: "Wow, you think you could take us to that spot?"

"Sure. But you'd have to lose the hat."

When it becomes obvious that Ekdahl's and my chuckling is the only reaction forthcoming, the guy goes whole hog, offering directions to his hot spots.

Ekdahl filed it all away, just in case the guy was telling the truth.

On Sunday, taking a breather from camp-breaking chores, Ekdahl, Jerry Dennis and I shared a few thoughts. As the acclaimed spearman/tracker for 1993, I felt empowered to confer an honor or two myself. And I anointed Ekdahl "shaman."

"Whoa, what am I, the assistant to Norris?" he asked.

"No," I replied. "Norris is shaman of the camp. You are shaman of the woods."

And he is.

Ekdahl has a wonderful way of telling stories so that no matter how detailed they are, you always are satisfied to have heard them. And he has a law enforcement officer's eye for detail. He has a wealth of experience in a variety of places, both with people and in nature. He has a Finlander's flair with the language that allows phrases like "conspiratorial step-in" to roll from his tongue without effort or apparent deliberation. Put these qualities together and you have someone who is expert at recreating the importance of the moment and at reminding us with mellow language of the reasons we meet in the woods each fall.

For example, on Saturday of camp, we split into two groups and headed for a common objective from opposite sides of the road. As his group approached mine, Ekdahl just sat on the side of a hill and listened. Finding birds became less important to him than mentally framing the experience for later narration.

Our excitement was obvious with our hoots and hollers getting louder and more prevalent as we neared him. Our excitement became infectious as we joined with the others who commenced with shouts of their own, equalling ours in pitch and intensity.

"After awhile, I remembered where I had heard a sound like that," Ekdahl said. "In late summer, when young coyotes are learning to hunt, they'll 'Yip! Yip!' like that. Pretty soon, they'll attract the attention of their elders who will join in the song."

So our little pack of hunters had behaved like coyotes, instinctively howling to our success.

I had enjoyed a particularly fine hunt with Lucy performing nearly flawlessly, pointing 15 of the 19 woodcock we flushed in an hour and a half. Norris and Jerry shot birds over her point as did I.

But as I sat in my truck and recorded our flush rates on my pocket calendar, memory suggested the date to be significant. With a little urging from an all-too helpful grief, I realized that exactly 10 years earlier my old setter Paddy, my first purebred hunting dog, had pointed his first woodcock. And grief took center stage for a few minutes. Until Ekdahl elbowed it aside.

His simple, insightful response was, "What better way to commemorate it than with the work Lucy turned in today?" A shaman sees things in ways others can't.

Ekdahl decided to accompany me as I left the woods for Marquette and a book signing. On the way, he asked what kind of a crowd I expected.

"Doesn't matter. After this morning, anything else good that happens would be like putting icing on Betty cakes."

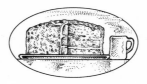

Dashing Through the Snow

JANUARY 1994

The word "surreal" seemed so precise that it grouted the scene's elements into a mosaic of memory. How interesting, I later found out, for the 20th century surrealist painter René Magritte once wrote, "The visible contours of objects in reality touch each other as if they formed a mosaic."

You're probably most familiar with Magritte's "The Son of Man," the painting of that guy in a derby with a green apple hiding his face. More intriguing is his painting of a dark-winged angel in a business suit leaning on a Paris bridge peering into the river as a lion reclines behind him gazing into the street. "Homesickness" it's called, and it presents the element which art historians tell us distinguishes surrealism: "the juxtaposition of incongruous objects."

So what was out of place in the scene I encountered this frigid Saturday morning, still more than an hour until daylight along I-94 just east of Benton Harbor. The storm belonged there because that's the job of an early morning snow storm. The winds belonged, for they were needed to make things more treacherous. The hawk belonged, for without him frozen in flight by the headlights for a fraction of a moment, that scene would have been as unremarkable as those of the previous hundred miles.

Perhaps surrealism's mandatory incongruity is explained by my reaction to the hawk as it retreated from the storm and headed into the woods: "What the heck am I doing here?"

This concept of "Tom as the disparate element in a southwestern Michigan Saturday morning white-out" became even more evident with my reaction to the next scene a few miles farther down the road: "Geez! Only an idiot would think of fishing on a day like this."

Pre-dawn's phantom daylight both enshrouded and highlighted the landscape below. Ice floes lazily cruised the St. Joseph River like pleasure craft in Port Huron the night before the race to Mackinac Island.

"Vague figures have a meaning as necessary and as perfect as precise ones," Magritte also wrote. And the frigid, shadowy stream precisely delivered a meaning that I ignored. I drove on.

Radio weather reports found no local temperatures above zero degrees and wind chills hovering around 20 below. I drove on.

I'd always wanted to see the dunes at the Warren Dunes State Park, so I followed I-94 to the exit, about 15 miles north of the Indiana border. Dawn was finally getting a grip on the day and elements of the landscape stood out like gray specters lining up along Main Street to welcome you to their ghost town.

Massive pine trees shook their fists at the storm. The dunes stood determined, the sand defying the snow it would eventually absorb. Sometimes, Nature vs. herself results in a stand-off.

I jumped out looking for signs of life in the park's headquarters. The storm allowed me to dash to the locked building, then like a cat toying with a mouse, smacked me just as quickly in the other direction. No stand-off here. I drove on.

On to the town of Three Oaks, where the movie *Prancer* was filmed in 1989. Now I've got to rent the dang thing. This place is so surreal that the pay telephone wouldn't accept our beloved, new area code when I called Maureen to let her know I was safe and sound—and freezing at the drive-up telephone that was situated so that the storm blew into the Suburban.

"Barger called at six," she informed me, "to cancel the trip."

Ron Barger of South Bend, Indiana, had been trying to lure me over for a couple of years. His promise of monster steelhead taken from a boat we'd launch in the St. Joseph River at Berrien Springs put me over the edge. Time was short, however, for Ron's wife Shelley is expecting their first child within the next couple of weeks. Last Saturday was the only date we could meet.

"Did you tell him I had left at four and that I still plan to catch a steelhead?" I asked.

"He said, 'Geez! Only an idiot would think of fishing on a day like this.'"

So I changed course and drove on.

Like the hawk had earlier, a flicker swished in front of the car and headed for the windbreak provided by a small stand of pines. At least I think it was a flicker. The tell-tale white rump was there, all right. But almost the entire back of its head was red, not just the little stripe. So it probably wasn't a flicker. That it was a red-bellied woodpecker, however, is even more improbable. So I settled on its being a flicker whose head feathers had been wind-burned.

Along M-60 just west of Jones, someone's handiwork graces a sign outside what I presumed was a meat packing plant. "People, Pork, Progress," it reads, and what puzzled me was not what kind of a mind creates such an inspirational slogan but what kind of a mind commissions it.

I drove on to the beautiful little town of Three Rivers. I had only seen it once before, more than seven years ago, and had remembered it as a quaint little burg that seems to represent Smalltown, USA. I neglected to note at the time, however, that construction could continue unrestrained along U.S. 131 while the historic downtown district can only add another veneer of olden days to the storefronts. I stopped for breakfast.

The chatty waitress (soon to be moving to Florida) with all the wisdom chiseled from her twenty-few years, dispensed work place philosophy to the middle age couple she was serving.

By the way, in case you are wondering, the three rivers are the Portage, St. Joseph and Rocky.

I wasted half an hour in Vicksburg looking for the VapoRub factory. And at the Kingman Museum of Natural History in Battle Creek, the most interesting exhibit is the snake skeleton displayed on the floor in the basement.

Eleven and a half hours and 495 miles after leaving, I returned the

Suburban to its berth in our garage.

That night, I dreamed of a massive steelhead hooked securely and fighting like mad. I started in my sleep, for the fisherman was built not unlike me.

But a green apple hid his face.

Without Women, Hear Us Roar

FEBRUARY 1994

S elf-respecting, lifelong members of the He-man Woman Haters Club (Outdoors Chapter) live by one simple canon: Unless they can otherwise point, flush or retrieve game birds, unless they will bait our hooks for us, unless they quit beating us in cribbage, NO GIRLS ALLOWED!

Now all we have to do is to find someone to inform the girls for us.

Last week, fellow club member Splash Westin called to finalize plans to cross country ski in the Pigeon River Country State Forest. Our annual winter get away, a couple of guys doing guy stuff with no girls to tell us we can't.

"Tom, did you get a weather report?" Splash asked.

"No. Why? What did you hear?"

"It's supposed to go down to 16 below on Friday night. You still want to camp out in the back of your Suburban?"

"Hold on a minute, Splash," I said and with the cordless phone in hand, jumped out of the bubble bath and dripped through the house until I found Maureen.

"Sixteen below, eh Splash? Boy, it's going to get pretty cold in the back of that truck," I said.

"You two are idiots if you sleep out in that kind of weather," Maureen said.

"Hey, Splash, Maureen says I have to stay in a motel."

"Yeah, Cindy Sue just told me the same thing," he answered.

When I picked up Splash on Friday afternoon, Cindy Sue asked when we expected to be home.

"Probably by three Sunday afternoon," Splash answered.

"You can stay later if you want," she said. "Just call."

There followed several minutes of silence as I drove us out of his subdivision, out of town and onto I-75. Then from behind the map book Splash mumbled, "I'll call you if I feel like callin' you."

I checked the rear view mirror just to be sure, then asserted, "That's right. She can't tell you what to do, Splash."

We exchanged high-fives and reveled in our freedom.

"But just don't tell Cindy Sue I said that, OK?"

"You got it, pal."

"In fact, you probably shouldn't tell her what you said, either."

"Roger!"

Hey! He-men keep secrets from the girls.

From the motel in the northern Michigan town of Vanderbilt, I called the forester, inquiring on the chance of our seeing elk as we skied the next day. "Not likely," he said, then added, "but my wife took the ten mile loop of the Shingle Mill Pathway a few days ago and saw a couple. You might want to try there."

Right. Like some girl is going to dictate our movements. We were he-men woman haters on a guy trip, making guy sounds, doing guy stuff and making guy choices. And we would decide all on our own where we would ski on Saturday.

"You sure you can handle a ten mile loop, Tom?" Splash asked the next morning as we forged ahead on the Shingle Mill Pathway.

"No problem, buddy," I said, flashing a "thumb's up." Besides, it was only 12 below, not 16.

At one point, nature summoned me to a campground outhouse. Enough snow had drifted against the door to force me to dig my way in. When I removed my skis to use one as a shovel, I sank up to my knees in the snow.

Inside, enough cold had gathered to steal my breath and hasten my motions.

"Boy, the girls sure wouldn't go for that," Splash commented upon my return as I hyperventilated myself back to operating temperatures.

He continued, "Yeah, they'd want some nice, comfy, warm place. Probably with a spa and a pool. A stocked bar in the—"

He caught himself then continued. "Better head out. Those elk aren't going to wait for us all day."

He was right. They didn't.

Later, as I hobbled out of an IGA grocery store with a tube of Ben Gay, Splash was finishing his check-in call with Cindy Sue. So, I thought I'd give Maureen the nod. Once she found out where we were and what we were planning, she started up again.

"You guys are idiots if you pay for another night in a motel when you are so close to the cabin."

"But it'll be cold there," I told her, in case she'd forgotten.

"Just ski in and build a fire. You'll be all right. Oh, and Tom,"

"What?"

"Make sure you sleep in the loft this time. Remember, hot air rises."

Splash and I both got quite a chuckle out of that one, like she actually thought we'd go soft on our weekend to rough it.

Soft, my eye. The toughest skiing of the day was the 200 yards from the end of the road up the driveway to our cabin which had been closed since Thanksgiving.

Inside the structure, conditions quickly deteriorated. My clothes were still damp after a complete cycle in the dryer. We couldn't find the cork screw for the wine. And the only way we could settle the quarrel was by agreeing that whoever got the chair closest to the fire had to relinquish my pile-lined slippers to the other.

I only had to ski out twice more that afternoon, once to retrieve the chocolate chip cookies from the truck, the other, to call Maureen again.

"OK. Now let's go over it one more time," she told me. "To get the color to work on the TV, you need to do what?"

"'Color Activate' button," I recited.

"Right. And no more cheese and crackers in the microwave."

"What if I use a pasteurized cheese food substitute?"

"Tom! The microwave didn't short out because of the type of

cheese you used! It's been sitting there freezing for three months! You can't just suddenly heat it up!"

So for dinner we ate cold cheese on cold crackers with no wine. Splash dispensed the goodies while I fiddled with the satellite dish. Fishing shows, World War II documentaries, action movies—we were ready for guy stuff.

"Boy, that Peggy Fleming can still skate, can't she, Splash? And look how fluid and soft she looks, especially in contrast to the hardness of the steel skates and the ice beneath her, I mean."

"You know," Splash added, "I felt pretty fluid out there on the trail today. My movements made me feel at one with my skis and the trail itself."

"I felt at one with the snow those three times I fell," I added.

"Yeah. And if I hadn't been so at one with my inner self of ski control, I would have fallen over you and we would have been at one with each other."

A pause, some eye contact—we shuddered at the implication then sprang into action. Splash searched the channels for a basketball game while I stepped outside to chop more firewood.

One of us slept in the loft that night.

Next year, we decided, girls would be allowed.

Well Within Limits

MAY 1994

A long the road, the snow-laden pine boughs sagged like the shoulders of old men on park benches.

Halfway to a spot in Presque Isle County, I was struck by the folly of it all when I mentally juxtaposed the green and brown camouflage I was wearing with the three inches of fresh, white snow in which I would be turkey hunting. So I returned to the cabin to take a Sunday morning nap.

The return on Saturday had been more exciting.

"Did you have a good time, Tom?" Maureen asked, bundled in a comforter and cozy before the fireplace.

"I saw a UFO."

"Oh no! Tom, don't tell anybody. Please."

I began to explain and Maureen settled into the type of resignation usually reserved for one of my JFK conspiracy theories.

Not having done any pre-season scouting, I had merely aimed the truck for a place where I was reasonably familiar with the roads and the topography. "If I get one, I get one," was my motto, and with my sore leg I wasn't planning on hiking long and far to find a gobbler.

Not fifty yards from where I parked, a grouse drummed passionately on his log. I had never heard drumming in the darkness before. But this one steadily performed, masking my sounds during his riffs so I could move closer and closer. Overhead, the enchanting music of a male woodcock making his courtship flights complemented the grouse's rhythm. A symphony for my ears only.

In the distance, about a half mile away, a couple of turkeys gobbled as they left their roosts. Not close enough, nothing to get excited about, so I focused on the grouse who was doing his best to call in a hen of his own.

When the turkeys got a little more lively, I backed off from the grouse and hobbled into the woods, finding a spot on a ridge which commanded quite a view of the surrounding territory.

Certain images accompany me on my turkey hunts, and I forget about them until they rush in at the appropriate times each spring. One is the image of El Sordo.

A character in Ernest Hemingway's *For Whom the Bell Tolls*, El Sordo is a rebel in the Spanish Civil War. In the best written chapter of the book, Sordo digs in on the side of a hill and, peering over the barrel of his automatic rifle, awaits his inevitable defeat with the gallant futility of a true Hemingway hero.

Likewise, I dig in awaiting my challenger. Only problem is, I can't sit still long enough to peer over my shotgun long enough. So, my defeat is inevitable, too.

The other memory is nudged by the song of the hermit thrush. And when I hear it, I think of Mozart. The hermit thrush has the most hauntingly beautiful call of the forest, one that's been described as "flute-like." And the first time I hear it each spring, I always wonder if Mozart could have written such a beautiful passage for *The Magic Flute*. And if so, if any human could have played it to such sublime effect.

Later that day, a teasing gobbler interrupted me as I consulted my new wildflower field guide to make my first identification: a trailing arbutus. And I actually left the gun in the truck while investigating some tracks I pronounced as those of a coyote. Common flower and track, yes, but you've got to start somewhere. And observations of that type are exactly what I had planned on making during my relaxed hunt this year.

What I hadn't planned on observing came while I answered the calls of those first two gobblers.

There I sat, dug in on the hillside, pointing the shotgun towards the valley like El Sordo. From the corner of my eye, I spotted movement in the southwestern sky. Sly turkey hunter that I am, I jerked my head around in time to see—something moving toward the southeast. The front oval part was a teal blue or turquoise and the tail, the traditional pale yellow or white light. It knifed through the sky just above the tree line for about five seconds, then dropped. A UFO.

I expected it to be an IFO (*Identified* Flying Object) as soon as the astronomy teacher at work, Tom Diliberti, analyzed the details I delivered. His closest conjecture calls it a meteor that hadn't totally burned upon entry into earth's atmosphere. But he couldn't be sure. And I don't have a field guide to cover such phenomena. Thankfully, art teacher Karen Drozdalski had seen a meteor before and confirmed my sighting.

The most impressive part of the experience was the self-possession of the object and the power which emanated from its silence as it calmly rushed through the air. I'd sensed the same thing twice before, once when hunting Canada geese for the first time and watching them handle the air currents with their wings as they prepared to land. The other was in the Atlantic Ocean while on a whale watching cruise. As the boat chugged along with its diesel rasping, the whale kept up effortlessly, an organic reactor certain it had plenty of power to spare. Power which emanated from the silence of the animal.

Ending my story I announced to Maureen, "I couldn't have asked for a better day."

"Even if you didn't get a turkey?" she asked, just to be sure.

"Doesn't matter."

Some of the best hunts end with neither game nor gun to be cleaned.

Spring Cleaning

I feel I think too much. Either that or I think I feel too much.

I'm confused.

The 18th Century English writer and politician Horace Walpole wrote, "The world is a comedy to those that think, a tragedy to those that feel." But the more walking around and thinking I think I'm doing, the more it seems, at least according to Walpole's way of thinking, that I am walking around and feeling. I think. As I said, I'm confused.

It all began with the first and only trip to the woodcock dancing grounds this spring. I'm sure we could have easily seen more had we undertaken more excursions, but once was enough and left me in too dark of a mood to return.

Right on cue, the bird greeted us with his *peents*—the nasal sounds like individual *beeps* from the cartoon Roadrunner—that signal his preparation for launching. And he lifted our spirits with several flights until we slipped from the field unnoticed, we assured ourselves, even by his gigantic eyes.

Then, just as quickly as the bird flutters to earth, my spirit likewise plunged, only deeper, when frank thoughts (feelings?) of mortality hit me. Not the egocentric types which whisper, "How in the world can this stuff continue if I die?" These were more plaintive in their realization: "This dance of the woodcock is so neat, an annual blessing, the confirmation of spring upon us. And if all goes well, it will continue long after I'm gone. I'm gonna' miss some of it. Rats!" Something like that.

I search my mind and recollect words from another time and place. William Cullen Bryant opens his classic poem, "Thanatopsis," with:

To him who in the love of Nature holds
Communion with her visible forms she speaks
A various language ...
... she glides
Into his darker musings with a mild
And healing sympathy that steals away
Their sharpness, ere he is aware.

Well, she certainly didn't steal away the sharpness of the dark musing I cogitated over on my way home from the woodcock singing ground. And it stuck with me.

Such dreariness has accompanied me in the north woods recently, in my unsuccessful forays for trout and morels. Turns out, I've spent more time behind the steering wheel than in the chilly stream with a fly rod or on a shadowed hillside with walking stick and mushroom bag. And when I drive, I lose myself in thought.

As I traveled the dusty, hot, forest roads, I was struck by how much I had become like the late John Voelker, known to millions as Robert Traver, the writer of *Anatomy of a Murder* as well as several books on fly fishing. Not that I had or ever will approach him in the quality of prose produced or the degree to which it gains public acceptance. No, this similarity was more of a realization that like him, I arise early and depart alone. I tour alone. I fish alone. Alone I am as I look for wildflowers or morels. And like him, I'm more at home with myself as I take myself down the dirt roads. Voelker, it is said, would travel ten miles out of his way on dirt roads to spare himself one mile on paved; the dust collected on the back windows of my Suburban implies the same of me.

The difference, of course, is that his solitude was voluntary, for there was no dearth of friends, companions or would-be acquaintances who would have gladly accompanied him. But he chose otherwise. In fact, in his famous "Testament of a Fisherman," he crows about how only in the woods he can "find solitude without loneliness." My solitude, on the other hand, begets loneliness, for it merely allows me more time to listen to myself, alone, and I'm getting weary.

This became all too clear on the most recent trip into the Pigeon River Country. Perhaps it is because I've read and watched *A River Runs Through It* too many times. Perhaps it is merely middle-age angst. But I felt compelled to sculpt some sort of family mythology revolving around trout fishing, dry fly fishing, of course, where none exists. Of all the passable trout streams in northeast Michigan, I chose the Pigeon. If I think about it, I realize the Pigeon flows into Mullet Lake, the only northern Michigan body of water my father and I ever shared.

I'm not a good fisherman. And my father never stalked trout with a fly rod, so try as I might to conjure up some magic in that stream that morning, it was just me alone, the water, no fish, and no history.

The mythology would have to limp along without gods or a hero.

As it turns out, I could have driven a shorter distance on better roads in less time and fished the mainstream of the Au Sable, but there the results are the same. Likewise on the Black, Thunder Bay and Ocqueoc rivers.

My casts become more and more urgent as I frantically try to entice disinterested trout and stir non-existent memories. I am reluctant to leave the stream for that means more driving and inevitably more loneliness.

Finally a teasing drizzle turns into a full-bore storm which hastens me to the truck as if I were a government witness leaving the courtroom. Rain and river water collect in the back of the truck where I've dumped my waders and jacket. My body heat immediately fogs the windows.

And seeping into my mind is the recognition that the tragedy of life is that one exists, ultimately, alone.

Self-pity begins to tap at my elbow.

But then hope sneaks up and nudges from the other side. It's packaged in the recollection of an unfinished thought from Voelker.

One day, along a dirt road on the way to his camp he stopped his woods truck, and with a spirit transcending the weight of age and experience he uttered, "I'm looking for something. ...."

After surveying the nearby landscape, he resumed driving, still on the lookout for something he either could not or cared not to articulate.

The heater soon dissipates the fog. The wipers smooth away the rain. Hope reminds me of the part of the Bryant quote about nature that my dark mood has conveniently allowed me to forget:

... for his gayer hours
She has a voice of gladness, and a smile
And eloquence of beauty ... "

A bit of nature, a taste of poetry and some ruminations from an old man: sometimes the most unlikely elements combine to fulfill the function of prayer.

A Coot Among Us

AUGUST 1994

Maureen checks her watch, double-checks the mounting trail of traffic behind us on the two-lane highway and heaves the kind of sigh that lets me know I'm in trouble.

"Jeepers, Tom! If you aren't going to go any faster, just pull over and let me drive."

"That won't be necessary, my dear," I advise. "I'll get us home safe and sound."

But she's already into her stride and doesn't lose a step.

"Look, Tom. You've got fifty yards between the road and the woods. It can't happen again. That really was a freak accident. What's the chance that you will slam the Suburban sideways into another tree?"

"Better safe than sorry," I patiently instruct.

"Tom! You're turning into a coot."

Fighting words.

"Look!" I say. "Just because I'm a cautious driver, you know, that doesn't make me a coot. So unless you have some other proof, I'll accept apologies starting now."

Her eyes lower, and I start feeling a little guilty for being so harsh on her. But doggone it, sometimes tough love is the only thing that works.

"Look at your shoes," she says, indicating the bone-colored loafers I had slipped off for the ride home.

"What about 'em?"

"They are a coot color."

"No way. You can't substitute 'coot color' for 'a classic summer tone in men's footwear'. So try again."

"OK. You're a coot because ... you can't let go of the past and you never throw out anything."

There follow several minutes of silence as I mentally inventory our house. Then it comes to me.

"What about last summer when I tossed away those polyester plaid flair pants. Hey baby. I'm hip to the groove. The '70s will never return."

"Neither will your 34-inch waist."

That crack doesn't count, not today anyway, because it doesn't include the word *coot*. Mistaking a technicality for an advantage, I press on.

"Seems like I'm up, two-zip. How's about trying to come up with another piece of coot evidence?"

"You said, 'how's about' just now."

"So what?"

"Coot talk."

"No way! You have to do better than that."

"All right," she says, as she rolls up her sleeves. "What about on our walk yesterday? Only a coot would wear those black socks with the white shoes and red shorts."

"Hey! Those are my specially padded hiking socks. Besides, we take half our walk in darkness."

"And we do the other half in daylight," Maureen proclaims, ready to take a victory lap.

"Oh yeah?" I carefully maneuvered her on this one. "If I'm such a coot, then how's come I was able to find my lost lunch bottle last week. I thought coots lose their memories."

"You did forget. You think I actually believed that someone stole the bottle then returned it to the counter in your office where you usually leave it?"

"Well, you said you believed me—"

"Quiet. I'm not done with your coot moves yet. What about when we went to see *Forrest Gump*?"

"No way. I couldn't help it. Those actors were talking too fast. I had to keep asking you—"

"No, no. I'm talking about before the movie during the previews," she says, then continues. "Tom, for fifteen minutes you kept saying the same two things over and over."

"What are you talking about?" I demand.

"'Ooooh! That looks like a good one,'" she mimics me.

"Well, those were enjoyable previews," I interject.

She parries with, "What about this: 'Boy! I really got these glasses clean this time. Look at that, would you Mo? Boy that old hanky really makes a good glasses rag.' What do you call that kind of talk, Tom?"

"But I'd never gotten them so clean before."

"You know who shares their pride in eyeglass cleaning with others?"

"Who?"

"Coots. And I'll tell you another thing."

"You really don't need to."

"Remember how you really liked that one style of shirt, so you bought it in three different colors? Guess who does that?"

"Somebody who's identified the fashion statement he wants to make," I declare.

"And yours says, 'Hey, look at the coot,' Tom. What else do I have to do to wake you up to the fact? You watched more figure skating this year than pro football. You talk to Nancy Kerrigan about weak spots in her routine as if she could hear you and you still marvel at that one skater you watched five years ago."

"Gary."

"What?"

"It was Gary Beechem. I really liked his style. He was fluid yet comical."

"Tom! You're a coot if you remember the names of non-gold medal-winning skaters. You even remember the guy's style! Take a look at yourself.

"You put more cream in your coffee than coffee. You refer to TV newscasters and talk show hosts by their first names as if they were your friends. You intentionally went out for a poached egg on toast this weekend. You only take me to restaurants where we get a discount if we order the dinner special before five o'clock. You insist on wearing those white pants with the rusty water stain across the front. You spent an hour yesterday organizing your key rings. And I've caught you lingering a bit too long at the *Lawrence Welk Show* when you are channel surfing. Coot City."

"I just want to see who Bobby's dancing partner is," I mutter, mostly to myself, for she might really have me this time. I mean, I am the one who, upon leaving to pick up some dry ginger ale, dutifully reported that I was heading out "for a bottle of *mix*." And I do tape *Matlock* if we're going out. I've decided that the next time we need a car, a used one will suit us just fine, that the depreciation on a new one is more than we need to bear. And if I'm honest, I'll admit that in the last couple of years, I've adopted the traditional *Whoy* to announce my plopping into a chair.

Worse thing is this cootness might be expanding in a negative fashion into my outdoor gear acquisition and expansion program which, heretofore, had flourished my entire adult life.

I have a seventeen-year-old spinning reel on which the drag is broken. Instead of following through when I should have, I talked myself out of justifying the expense of a new one. After all, it's not like I can't make do with the classic model, I reasoned.

And I've given up buying new lures because I have plenty.

Same thing with clothes. Instead of buying a new chamois shirt, I've decided my old one is good enough even though the collar is so tattered it's unraveling.

Instead of buying fishing shoes with special deck soles, I figured my basketball shoes could serve double-duty. Then came the groin pull which lingered from the first basketball game of the season in November well into the following July. Coots refuse to acknowledge when to hang it up, according to Maureen. I'd play again, but I've already ruined the shoes while fishing, so I guess I'll just retire.

And this is the first year that the fall hunting edition of the mail order catalogues could not inspire me to try something new. I have the urge to hold out for a *Sans-a-belt* version of "brush tuff" waterproof hunting pants.

Hold out ... double-duty ... plenty ... justify ... make do—when did those terms sneak into my vocabulary? My head spins with the implications.

Finally, Maureen breaks the silence. "You aren't falling asleep already, are you? Why don't you pull over so we can change drivers."

I quietly do what I am told.

"Whoy," I utter, plopping into the passenger's seat like a contented cow just in time for her nap. I couldn't have planned it any better.

Plus with Mo at the helm, we'll get home in plenty of time for Lawrence Welk.

The Forever Question

Why do we hunt?

The response to that simple, straightforward question probably reposes at the core of most serious discussions among hunters each fall, from duck blinds to deer camps, in cabins, saloons and around campfires.

Surely some people hunt for the opportunity to bag some game animals that they enjoy eating. But the concept of subsistence sport hunting is a contradiction. So, other than to put a little meat on the table, hunters today must hunt for additional reasons.

What are they?

It's occurred to me that our reasons are really emotions, that we head to the woods more to satisfy deep feelings than to address logical concerns.

Look up the verb *hunt* in any dictionary and you will find among the definitions, "to search, seek."

Instead of "Why do we hunt," therefore, a more precise question might be, "In addition to the game animals, what emotions do we seek when afield?"

Certainly a sense of tradition draws many of us to the woods. The last two weeks of November provide us an excuse to partake in one of the closest things we have in our society to ritual: deer camp. But it could just as easily be woodcock camp or waterfowl camp earlier in the fall if we've done these long enough for rituals to have evolved.

What matters is that the Olympia Stadium has been torn down and

Gordie Howe has retired. Also, a year without a World Series has forced fans to capitulate to the notion of baseball as nothing more than big business. Apprentice thugs have swiped the glee from Halloween trick-or-treating. Thanksgiving parades and holiday bowl games now come shrink-wrapped in corporate logos. And the face of traditional America has been scratched and gouged by the hand of a modern America strung out on the drugs of greed, quick fixes, intolerance and finger pointing.

Traditions have retreated from our lives, but the need for them remains in the front lines of our spirits. That's why some of us can feel snug in the knowledge that during the night of every November 14, we will be nestled in the arms of a camp where some things— the activities, the stories, the excitement—remain intact as long as we breathe life into them.

Such security also gives way to an appreciation of the past that might otherwise escape younger people and which might grant additional comfort to older people feeling the crush of a world gone modern. Chances are good that somewhere this week a grandson with his portable CD player and straw-yellow or purple bleached hair will be using a rifle passed along to him by his granddad. And if he's lucky and the old man is sensible, some knowledge and some history will have figured in the transferral of the property.

When the boy bags his first buck, perhaps the fire in his spirit will thaw more memories for the old man, thoughts of a black and red plaid wool outfit, a JON-E hand warmer, kill tags made of metal bands and a hunting knife with an authentic stag horn hilt.

Having delivered a little of the past, the old man might now sense more than the mere blood link between himself and the youngster whose fleeting attention span was spawned by music videos and who can navigate the Internet more adeptly than the old man can cruise the lawn on his riding mower.

Some of us hunt because it allows us to move beyond a world of concrete, airline commercials and talk radio and to maintain some kind of a connection with the natural world that we love. Moreover, if dogs are our passions, we seek to enhance that connection and to forge a tighter bond, a sense of teamwork with our best buddies who would otherwise just be pets.

Still others of us hunt for the challenge of matching wits with nature. Hunting allows us the opportunity to test our knowledge, skills and instincts to whatever degree we wish to take a risk with nature.

In a world where traffic flow is constantly constipated by the combination of increased volume, detours and lane closures; where workers can only suffer in silence the humiliating orders issued by dispassionate bosses who, with their eyes glued squarely on their career tracks, have learned to command but not to lead; where tax assessors merely grin, nod and deny our requests; hunting allows us a sense of control. We decide from which direction to hunt a grouse covert. We decide how we'll set the duck decoys and when to let the calls dangle around our necks in silence. We decide on the best spot for intercepting a big buck. We decide when to set the hounds onto a rabbit. In short, if only briefly, hunting gives us a say in matters that matter to us.

We hunt in order to create personal and communal histories that can be relived in vivid images and thus become our personal and communal mythologies.

Finally—and this might actually be a by-product and not a reason—hunting confronts us with and forces us to accept a reality unique to our humanity: in a world where nature shows no pity, we are the only predators consciously bearing the weight of the knowledge that we will eventually become prey.

I'm saddened when I find baby birds in our yard in spring, dead or nearly so. Nothing I can do will help them and nature will see to it that they die slowly, in agony.

"So it's all right for you to shoot them but not for them to just die?" my wife Maureen asked without a hint of sarcasm, sincerely trying to understand why such a seemingly minor tragedy would cause tears in my eyes.

"No, that's not it. It has nothing to do with what's right or wrong. It just has to do with what is," I paused for a moment, "and that is the sad part."

Hunters play a role in nature at its most basic, tragic level. I've never heard a hunter say he or she feels good about the killing. Most say they feel bad for the animals they've killed. Ultimately, we also feel bad for ourselves knowing that the day will soon come when the earth will no longer feel the tread of our boots. Yet, oxymoron or not, it's in the fall of the year when, seduced by October, hunters feel most impassioned.

In his poem "Easter 1916," William Butler Yeats describes Ireland after the uprising against the English with the chorus, "All is changed, changed utterly: a terrible beauty is born." Perhaps that line best articulates the ultimate emotion hunters encounter, whether they seek it or not.

If you could for a moment on a golden autumn morning sense your entire being—body and soul—tremble as you approach a likewise trembling setter on point in the alders, then you'd sip this cider that is the act of hunting.

If you could then seize the moment at which you precipitate the tragedy, you'd also grasp the instant and utter genesis of a terrible beauty.

As in the poem.

As in real life.

At Home, in the Woods

U sed to be when I'd head out for some bird hunting, Maureen and I'd share an exchange that went something like this: "Mo, I'm going bird hunting ... Maureen?"

Since the advent of Lucy the English setter as Maureen's home buddy and Tom's woods pal, the exchange has been amended to this: "Mo, I'm going hunting."

"OK. Don't let anything happen to Lucy."

We must have transcended to a new level, for just recently, the day after Christmas as a matter of fact, she showed new concern for me as I announced, "Mo, I'm going hunting."

"You idiot! You're going to kill yourself out there."

"Whaddya' mean, Maureen? I'm super cautious when I go out. For me, hunting is as safe as a day at home."

"That's what I'm afraid of."

"What are you talking about?"

"Tom! Just think about it. How did you get your last three injuries?"

"Well, I threw out my back shoveling the snow—"

"That was weeks ago! I'm talking about within the last week."

Even though she had narrowed things down for me, I was stumped.

"Let me help you remember," she said. "First, you scraped open your finger while raking the loose hair from the dogs. Then you bruised your shoulder and dislocated your thumb when you fell down while trying to get out of your chair in your office."

"You know, that stumps me. It's a real mystery. I still don't understand how my foot got tangled in the computer cords and telephone wires. I guess you might say I got wrapped up in my work, eh? Ha!"

Maureen wasn't laughing.

"And how did you pull your groin? At that wedding, dancing to the 'Y.M.C.A.' song. And you think it's safe to walk around in the woods with a loaded rifle?"

"It's a loaded shotgun," I should have told her but instead I took the smart way out: "Well, Carole said she'd never seen anyone do the marching part of the song with so much gusto."

Maureen merely shook her head and replied, "Just don't let anything happen to Lucy."

Under normal circumstances I wouldn't be hunting grouse this late in the year. But three omens told me it would be OK to do so.

First, I'm a terrible shot and have only taken two December grouse my entire life.

Second, the mild weather the previous three days had been so inviting as if to ordain that Lucy and I hit the woods.

The weather on those three previous days turned very predictable: early morning fog burned away before noon leaving the rest of each day bathed in sunlight. Temperatures flirted with the 50 degree mark.

The third omen was simple: I'd stayed home on those warm days before Christmas because I could just as easily slip away on Monday when the weather was predicted to be even better and when everyone else would return to work.

As a result, Monday morning found me not barreling into Lapeer County but casually sipping coffee at the Shamrock Pub in Utica.

"Watcha' got planned for today?" owner Joe Mayernik asked.

"Goin' huntin', Joe," I responded.

(Away from Maureen, I am free to omit the final *g* in *i-n-g* words without takin' any heat, you see.)

"Getting kind of a late start, aren't you, pal?" Joe asked.

"No way. I've got a plan. Just gotta' wait for the fog to burn off."

In stomped Sandy the bartender, muttering to herself and frowning almost worse than Joe does on a bad day. Then she erupted for all to hear.

"You know we're the only place that's open today, Joe? I kept pinching myself to see if I really had to come in today when the rest of the world has the day off."

Joe nodded in sympathy and responded, "Better clean the ketchup bottles first."

"What does she mean, that you're the only place open, Joe?" I asked.

"Just about every place is closed so the people get a long weekend for the holiday."

"Gotta' go," I said, spinning from my stool.

"What about waiting for the fog to burn off?" Joe asked.

"No time."

By the time I reached my secret spot, it was too late.

No, the fog was still there, for the temperature would only rise to the high 30s. It was too late because the spot obviously is not a secret.

Every turn-out near every decent grouse hunting locale at the Ortonville Recreation Area held at least one vehicle. And why not? Everybody except Sandy had the day off. Surely some of those people were grouse hunters.

I finally located a place to park, along a dirt road that threatened with both ice and mud. I had never hunted this spot before. If I had, I wouldn't have left the truck on this day.

The uneven topography forced a march up and down lots of hills. "Pop!" There goes the groin.

In the low areas, vines as thick as computer cables lasso my legs and launch me earthward. "Smack!" go the thumb and shoulder again, upon impact. On my way down, I flail for a handhold only to grasp a stalk covered with needle-sharp pickers. "Zip!" sings this finger shredder.

Not long thereafter, I am safe at home in robe and slippers, sipping hot chocolate into which Maureen has dropped an ice cube so I won't burn my tongue.

"Want to play some cribbage?" she asks.
"No, I don't think I should," I reply.
"Whatsa' matter? You afraid of losing again?"
"No."
"Then what are you afraid of?"
"Paper cuts."

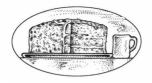

Mr. Grouse Talks Turkey

MAY 1995

In silence, Les Zimmerman and I took our places at the table, clasped our hands, and bowed our heads in contemplation.

Like ascetics we had arisen well before dawn. But we weren't emulating monks and we weren't saying grace.

Rather, our invocation would have sounded something like, "Give us this day our daily bird—or at least a chance to work him."

Our open-air altar, a picnic table, sits in the hills of southwest Pennsylvania at a strategic spot where two ridge lines meet. We perched upon it with our hearts, spirits and ears attuned to the bird in question, the wild turkey. Given the appropriate oral cue, we could quick-step towards either of two hollows, the depressions too narrow to be called valleys, which sag between hills like hammocks.

Two months earlier, Les, of nearby Washington, Pennsylvania, got my blood boiling hotter than that of a lecherous gobbler on the trail of his third hen of the morning.

"You've got to come down and hunt Greene County with us sometime, Tom," he said. "It's got the greatest turkey population of any county in the nation."

He continued his long-distance seduction with, "Last week during a rain storm I counted 165 of them in one field."

I stopped short of a triple-gobble, just in time to ask if I could bring a friend.

Norris McDowell had never hunted turkeys before but he lathered up when he heard about Greene County with the greatest turkey population in the nation.

Time for a road trip.

Les's pal Ray Jennings, an expert turkey caller, opted to shepherd Norris on his quest. Off they went well before 5:00 each morning, returning sometime after the noon quitting time, Norris having engraved his boot tread on every hill and hollow within three miles of Hickory Hill Farm.

Though Les has gained permission to hunt over 1,000 acres, his Hickory Hill comprises only 20. And for the last thirty-five years he's leased an additional 40 which he's turned into a preserve managed for ruffed grouse. In fact, he's done so much work on behalf of grouse in that part of the country that when time came for the U.S. Postal Service to issue stamps featuring the fifty state birds, the Pennsylvania painting was based on a photo taken from one of the several blinds "Mr. Grouse" has built on his preserve.

"Those are 'Les-sized' blinds, too, you'll notice," said Les's other pal, Merritt Downing. At about six foot three and over 200 pounds, Downing knows the strain of trying to squeeze himself into those blinds that are built to hold Mr. Grouse comfortably. Les, you see, is about five foot four maybe weighing 140 pounds if he's wearing a hunting vest stuffed with high brass shells.

"If you think about it a little, he kind of resembles a grouse," Ray told Norris.

The dark, skittish eyes flit from object to object as quickly as his thoughts dart from subject to subject. Les is constantly on the move. Such nervous energy accounts for his continual surveillance of and reaction to his surroundings. And it shows itself in his chatter and banter and patter, except when he is in the woods in hot and quiet pursuit of those Greene County turkeys.

His legs are so short that he can't find hunting pants in the appropriate length. About halfway between his ankle and calf you'll notice his solution: safety pins. Les is in his early 70s yet he conquers the ridge tops and hollows with the speed and grace of a young DiMaggio and the silence of a grouse giving someone the slip.

"Les, during the war, were you in the infantry?" I manage to gasp, trying to keep up.

"I was with the Corps of Engineers but we worked with the infantry. Why?"

"Never mind. I'll just take bigger steps."

Such energy occasionally plays him false.

Seeking a vantage from which to ambush some turkeys he's noticed in the distance, Les has just charged past the spot where Merritt had set his hunting vest. He's also managed, however, to entangle a four-foot strand of barbed wire with his pant leg. The wire, in turn, has snagged Merritt's vest. Down the path head the man, the wire and the vest, Les not noticing until he's physically halted by Merritt's hand on his shoulder.

"Les, you've just got to slow down," says Merritt, normally as laconic as Les is talkative.

Without missing a step as he traverses the trails he's worn onto the ridges, Les kicks aside any twigs or fallen limbs a hunter might otherwise crack in a pre-dawn gambit to outflank a gobbler.

Heading up the ridge from the small hunting cabin on the property, Les adjusts his cap and gives it a tug as he passes the white crosses marking the graves of Hickory Hill Rocky and Red Baron, his first two hunting dogs.

Whether he's prompted to do this by an itch, a reflex or the memory of his fine setters is immaterial. The action suggests another of Zimmerman's qualities, one with which the ever-active, constantly alert grouse cannot be imbued: his sentimentality. It's exhibited in the poems and literary excerpts he's matched with appropriate artwork, framed and hung in a special corner of his wildlife art gallery back in Washington. It's displayed in camp through a mish-mash of memories: photos, letters, dog collars, jars of egg shells from grouse and turkey nests, a "Pennsylvania State Bird" sign, whitetail antlers and turkey wing feathers and a nature area named after a departed comrade.

Alas, except for a Betty cake and a ham, Norris and I left no such mementos in camp. For in the county with the greatest population of wild turkeys in the nation, the birds failed to respond to Ray's calls,

Norris' hopes, Merritt's patience or the humble supplications
uttered by Mr. Grouse and me.

Most Dangerous Games

JUNE 1995

I'm fast coming to the conclusion that if it weren't for my participation in physical activities, I'd be in pretty good shape.

Basketball, the love of my life, has been particularly brutal. The bookend injuries are when Larry Hoste bit me in the back of the head in eighth grade while I was attempting a put-back after a rebound and when I pulled my groin in April of 1994. The doctor thinks that if I take it easy during the summer and don't split any firewood at the cabin or try to break up any concrete slabs at home, the groin ought to be almost healed for the last few weeks of bird season this year.

Sandwiched between those are countless ballooned ankles and back spasms which drive me to my knees. My buddy Joe at the Shamrock Pub once sprained my little finger giving me a "hard high five" in celebration of the second of our eventual five consecutive championships. Three days later, my hand had swelled to the size of a healthy sweet potato; to this day, the finger still winces under pressure.

Also, football snared me during our senior year in high school. At an early season workout without pads or helmets, future All-Pro lineman Joe DeLamielleure dug his cleats into the ground during a "bear crawl" drill on all fours. Only problem was that I had gotten a body length behind him and instead of the ground, his cleats dug into the back of my head, not far from the scar commemorating the misalignment of Larry Hoste's teeth. A couple weeks later, during the pre-season scrimmage, my ribs took a bruising from what would now be an illegal crack-back block, and my shin developed a puncture wound and an eventual abscess from what has always been an illegal spiking from an opponent trying to slow me down. And during its first week of practice with the Brown University freshman team, my left elbow garnered a bone chip which remains to this day.

Nailed from behind during a touch football game one frigid January day, I split my lip on the shoulder of the guy I was chasing, tearing forever that curtain of skin which holds the upper lip to the gums. And in a pick-up hockey game, I took a half dozen stitches after someone's stick creased the edge of my temple.

Baseball delivered 11 more near the other eye when I overran a pop-up and the ball broke my sunglasses—during warm-ups, no less. And I'm afraid only time will confirm the degree of ruin I brought to my knee while blocking the plate as a catcher for our softball team.

I've damaged my other knee while loosening up to exercise and notched a scar on my heel from where a speedboat nearly severed my Achilles tendon while I snorkeled in the Bahamas. I've had to lay off my fitness walks because of blisters, and about two minutes before giving up mountain biking, I actually thought I was doing a smart thing, trying to forearm a tree out of the way. And don't even get me started on the golf cart injury.

All this is prelude to the idea that my most recent hurt should come as no surprise. Even I, however, find this one hard to believe.

"So where ya' been, Tom?" Joe asked when, for the first time in over a month, I stopped into the Shamrock for my usual Saturday coffee last week.

"Busy, Joe. Big doin's," I replied.

Nodding toward the black brace around my wrist, he asked, "You get into a summer hoop league or something?"

"No, Joe. This is a new one. I sprained it fishing."

"What did you do, catch Moby Dick and your wrist gave way?"

Joe was pretty pleased with himself because he knows how much I love the classics. But that wasn't it.

Outdoor communicator Mark Gomez of Ferndale had invited me along to jig for walleyes in the lower Detroit River. As usual, his patter on the ride down consisted mostly of expressions of joy at the wonderful weather conditions and of hope for the great fishing we were sure to enjoy. What do I know? I'll believe anyone willing enough to take me along.

Well, Mark caught the first, the most, and the biggest, but the only legal size fish he netted was a five-inch rock bass. He also hooked a walleye and smallmouth bass, both undersize.

At least I caught a legal walleye. But my joy was abbreviated, for I had to horse the fish in quickly so I could help Mark with his monster catch. Working a 3/8 ounce jig-head tipped by a minnow, Mark had been greeted by a 38-inch, 14-pound muskie. Yet even if the season had been open, that monster fish was too small.

About ten minutes later, using the same jigging method, I caught my first muskie ever, though it was nowhere near the size of Mark's. No need to worry about a sprained wrist there.

"Well, did you get it while holding up a stringer of fish?" Joe asked.

"No. We didn't keep any."

"Then how?"

Ah, truth, the moment I dreaded.

"I sprained it while riding in the boat."

"What! What kind of an idiot sprains his wrist on a boat ride?"

"Geez. You sound just like Maureen did when I called from the emergency room."

Gomez has a bass boat. The river was choppy. He had to get up on plane in order to make headway. We bounced so much I braced myself to protect my back. After all, I didn't want a repeat of the golf cart injury. I came down on the wrist at an odd angle.

The rest, for five weeks now, is history.

"Only you, Tom, only you," Joe said.

"Tell me about it. Oh well. Hey, how about a fill-up on this coffee?"

"Sure. But do me a favor," he said, pushing my arms to my sides.

"What's that?"

"My liability premium is overdue. I don't want you handling the cup."

"Well, what should ... how am I ..."

He offered me a straw.

Sanctuary

If you spend enough time and make enough of an effort to establish a relationship with a piece of literature, an interesting phenomenon occurs. Instead of reading it and recollecting scenes from life, you will navigate through the scenes and recognize the literature.

"Let us spend one day as deliberately as Nature," Henry David Thoreau writes in *Walden*. That thought has rested comfortably on the shelf of my intellect for over a quarter of a century. Only last week did it begin to reverberate in the background of experience.

The occasion was my spending a week at our cabin in northern Michigan. As you know, full-time I am a high school teacher. School had just let out for the summer, and after a maelstrom of a year, the only thought on my mind was *retreat*. While I have loafed there for as long as ten days at a stretch, this was the first time I used the cabin as a hideout, the first time I headed north seeking sanctuary.

Our little nest provides a few more creature comforts than Thoreau enjoyed in his one-room shack at Walden Pond. Yet the longer I lingered there, the more the simple, natural details rose, like cream, to the surface of my consciousness. Attention to those details helped me to live "deliberately" as Thoreau did, with my aching spirit convalescing in nature's embrace.

Each morning, as the birds tuned up for daylight, Lucy my English setter and I arose for our walk through and around town. I carried a shillelagh in case any unchained, overly aggressive dogs needed to be discouraged from greeting us with their teeth. Every time during the last half mile, however, my happy pace determined that instead of bearing a cudgel, I should be slipping along with a walking stick. So the shillelagh changed the focus of its attention and the angle of its carriage.

A morning cup of coffee, something I simply don't make time for back home, preceded twenty minutes of quiet time. Technically it's not meditation, but that's the closest word I can use without going into great detail. I'd park myself on the porch in a tilt-back chair with Lucy on my lap. Bathed in sunlight and serenaded by various birds, I'd sit back, close my eyes, breathe deep and try my best to clear my mind.

That simple morning exercise shapes the state of mind that Thoreau seems to be talking about when he writes, "To him whose elastic and vigorous thought keeps pace with the sun, the day is a perpetual morning." I would open my eyes, relaxed, refreshed, aligned with the morning. The key, I believe, is to unwind before getting wound up.

My day would end as the sun's heavy eyelid drooped in the western sky and the birds chirped adieu to its light.

Throughout the day, with basic survival assured, I was free to attend to the wonderful lessons offered by nature, a more gloriously interactive educational tool than you'll ever find on the Internet.

On the pond, Canada geese had raised their goslings nearly to adulthood. Hen mallards supervised broods that spanned in age from youngsters to juveniles. In the woods, some young woodcocks had been able to fly for a month. And ruffed grouse chicks, traditionally late hatchers, were stumbling through a hastened childhood. According to nature's timetable, then, the spring's activity should have been completed at the two wood duck boxes I'd hung.

A check in one showed two eggs, neither hatched. Inside the second were eight eggs and a dead chick. The DNR's local wildlife technician helped determine that most likely something had happened to the female before she could complete incubation on the other eggs. Of course, in matters of nature, one cannot be absolutely sure. But nature is often brutal to her own.

Similarly, a couple of massive snapping turtles had laid eggs on the soft sandy beach two doors down from us. Within two days, raccoons had located the eggs and destroyed the nests.

On the other hand, I was able to step in to rescue painted turtles at least a half dozen times. They like to migrate from the tiny pond to the bigger one. But they don't take the outlet culvert beneath the road; they crawl overland. After seeing one squished turtle, I decided to become a relocation assistant for any more headed towards the edge of the big pond.

A certain amount of freedom accompanies the realization that you can sit around in beat-up moccasins and an old sweatshirt until the spirit moves you to take a ride through the woods. There, it won't be long until you spot deer and wild turkeys as well as elk. Yet from the porch you can often watch the bald eagle scanning the pond for lunch. Or the mama mallard scolding the loon that approaches too closely to her brood. The loon, seemingly oblivious to the racket, merely dips its head below the water in search of a meal.

This freedom both shoos away those concerns that drag you down and, because you have a close relationship with the book, brings to mind yet another thought from *Walden*: "I know of no more encouraging fact than the unquestionable ability of man to elevate his life by a conscious endeavor."

Sometimes a consciousness of nature is all it takes to begin the ascent.

Rat Trapped

JULY 1995

You can tell I'm an outdoors guy because Maureen uses animal terms to describe me.

Things like "huggy bear ... filthy pig ... dirty cur."

She says I "grouse" or "carp" about things, that I "badger" her during "Wheel of Fortune," and that when it comes time to help with dishes I play "possum." And because she has an interest in English Romantic poetry, she'll frequently call me a "graybeard loon" borrowing from Samuel Taylor Coleridge's *Rime of the Ancient Mariner*. I ask if she'd consider me a card "shark" when we play cribbage.

"No, but I consider you a coot all the time," she responds.

Hey. *Coot*. That's one I haven't heard in a while.

More recently, her refrain has been, "Tom, you're nothing but a pack rat."

No sense arguing. I have so much trouble parting with things that I had to build a special "stuff" room in our basement. But a problem arises through our mutually exclusive definitions. According to Maureen, stuff is merely apprentice *junk*; after three years, out it goes. When I say, "stuff," however, I mean, "something I don't ever want to throw out because as soon as I do I'll need it and have to go buy a new one."

"You remember what you promised when we bought the cabin," she told me recently on the third anniversary of our purchase. "This junk has got to go. What about the canoe?"

OK. OK. It's not like I planned on owning a fleet of three canoes. I just had to make sure that I wouldn't need the one that came with the cabin.

"I'll sell it in a garage sale," I mumbled in meek response.

"When?"

"Soon."

"It had better be sooner than that, Tom, or I'll throw out all this junk when you go to woodcock camp."

Pretty serious threat. But camp isn't till October, so at least I have some lead time.

"So what else will you get rid of," she pressed. Man, she is relentless.

"I don't know."

"How many shotguns do you have now, four?"

"Well, I think it's six."

"What! Do you really need all of them?"

"Sure. I've got my first string grouse gun. And I can't get rid of the back-up because Jerry borrows it every year for camp. Then there's my turkey gun. Plus the spare over and under twelve gauge. I started using the .410 last year for rabbit. And the sixteen gauge single shot that my uncle left me. Oh yeah, the black powder gun."

"That's seven," she announced.

"When did you get so quick at word problems?"

Before I had a chance to recover she came at me again.

"How many fly rods do you have now?"

"Does that count the one that I won in the drawing at the writers conference but it hasn't been delivered yet?

"Just tell me how many you have right now."

"Four."

"You're not even any good with a fly rod. You told me that yourself. But I suppose you need all of them."

"Of course I do. The new one might be iffy because it's a six weight which means it can take five, six, or seven weight line. And I do have the five which can take four, five, or six weight line. And the big one is an eight which means it can take seven, eight, or nine. So, you see there is some overlap. But what am I supposed to do, refuse a free—"

"I DON'T CARE ABOUT ALL THAT! The point is, the new one is just going to add to the clutter. You've got to get rid of something else."

"OK, I'll sacrifice the big tent."

"That's no big deal because you've only used it three times in five years."

"Yeah, but you never know when I'll need it again."

She reminds me I also promised to get rid of the tons of extra pots and pans we brought back from the cabin when we pulled the ol' switch of replacing our cookware at home and moving the old set to the cabin.

"Except I want to keep that one frying pan and the steamer," I reminded her.

"Get rid of them!"

OK. OK. I'll just wait till she's not looking and stash them.

"I don't trust you, Tom," Maureen said. "You're probably going to wait until I'm not looking and stash them. You need to get rid of something now."

Oh-oh. The noose began to tighten. I quickly surveyed the rest of the basement to the areas where my stuff had migrated from its overpopulated homeland.

Finally my eyes fell upon the hat rack.

"OK, Mo. I'll tell you what. I'll get rid of most of my baseball caps over there."

"This I've got to see," she said.

For the longest time, I've been a real sucker for caps. Any kind, just about any logo. College caps, pro teams, companies that manufacture some good stuff. It really doesn't matter; if the cap is available, I'll grab one.

My favorite caps I save for appropriate outdoor activities. Once I find new favorites, I move the old ones down the scale to work caps which come in two categories. First-stringers are for general work during which I might sweat and the hat might get dirty: yard work, minor plumbing repairs, climbing into the attic to inspect the insulation. Second-string caps are assigned to activities that might get them dirty and wrecked; usually those tasks include my sliding beneath a vehicle or a handling a torch. Sometimes both.

On the surface, I had assigned myself a tough job. But what Maureen didn't realize is that I've got three more boxes of caps stashed somewhere in the junk room.

Let's start with the college caps. OK. These can go: Notre Dame, SMU Mustangs, New Mexico State, Vanderbilt, plus this University of Michigan road kill I had found. Texas Christian stays because it has the same initials as I do. West Point reminds me of the student whom I'd recommended, so that stays, and so do the three Brown University caps which remind me of my college football days.

The Tigers cap is a remnant from 1984 and those glory days—like an Ernie Harwell-called home run—are "long gone." It's outta' here.

The Phillies cap is a souvenir of our baseball tour to different ball parks in 1982 and the night I walked the streets of Philadelphia waiting for my buddy to pick me up and talking to myself so that the muggers, thinking I was a crazy man, would leave me alone. It worked. It stays.

I love the logo for Irish Setter Boots, so those three caps stay.

A man cannot possess too many blaze orange hunting caps so all eight stay. So does the ratty old white one bearing the Johnson Reels logo. That's a classic and filthy as it is, it remains my fishin' cap.

"Tom, that's only six caps you've gotten rid of," said Maureen in dismay.

"Gee, honey, at least it's a start," I said giving her my patented bottom lip quiver.

"You're right, dear. That's a very nice gesture on your part. It shows you're really trying."

"But of course."

"And that wasn't so bad was it," she asked.

"Not really," I said, still pouting so she'd think I had gone through a real ordeal.

"Good. Because that was only the beginning."

"What?"

"Let's see how many pairs of hunting boots you can get along without."

"But—"

"Then we'll tackle your tackle box. Hey, that's a good one, don't you think? HA!"

"That's not funny."

"After that," she said, handing me an old friend she meant to evict from my boot pile, "we'll see what we can do about those other hats I found in those three boxes in the stuff room."

Rats!

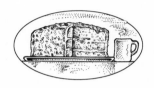

Night Vision

SEPTEMBER 1995

*U*pon *a darkened night*
The flame of love was burning in my breast
And by a lantern bright
I fled my house while all in quiet rest

So go the opening lines to "The Dark Night," which Canadian singer Loreena McKennitt adapted and set to music in 1994. The original eight-stanza poem was written in 1578-79 by the Spanish monk, St. John of the Cross. On the surface it seems a simple yet simply eloquent love poem. The lover slips away from the house and into the night to meet her beloved. Throughout the other stanzas, their relationship grows more intense. It's that simple.

Apparently there's more, however. For John also wrote a 52-page commentary on the poem. In it he deals not with romantic love but with the love between a person and his God, similar to that portrayed in the "Song of Songs" from the Old Testament.

As John explains it, the dark night, ominous and negative as it sounds, is basically the aridity or "dry spell" one passes through on his way to enjoying spiritual enlightenment and a more intense relationship with his God. His basic premise is that, as in a human relationship, the only way to achieve transcendence and unity is through absolute trust of and surrender to the beloved. But first one must deny himself those appetites which hold him back. Such denial usually leads to uncertainty and the darkness. Thus, finding oneself adrift in the dark night is not a sign of abandonment; rather, it's an indication of steady, though perhaps indistinct, progress. Trusting the night is the first step towards redefining the relationship.

Some modern psychologists borrow from John and apply the term to the essential darkness or emotional dry spells through which we sometimes must wander before enjoying psychological enlightenment and more intense insight into our own lives.

Both interpretations teach that the darkness is not to be feared. Rather, we should embrace it as it guides us with a torch of its own, a more loving friend perhaps than the clear light of day.

I've embraced a dark night of my own.

Upon this darkened night, anticipation teased and tugged within. Long before dawn, I slipped from the cabin and followed the quivering beam of the tiny flashlight to the canoe while Maureen and the pups remained inside at rest.

Upon that misty night
In secrecy, beyond such mortal sight
Without a guide or light
Than that which burned so deeply in my breast

I paddled through the night into the mist that cupped me in its hands. As quietly as I could, I guided the canoe to the river channel. Downstream about a mile, a dam stitches the river and stanches its flow. As a result, my waters seem more like a pond than a stream. Lily pads, tree stumps, and other vegetation clog the shallows, so paddling is easier in the deeper waters of the channel.

I point the canoe upstream. My paddle strokes—tight, silent, deep and effective—convey my secret to the water as the cabin lags farther and farther behind.

In such utter darkness, an eerie sense of suspension taps my shoulder as my body perceives movement that my eyes cannot confirm. It jogs the decades-old memory of my first trip across the Mackinac Bridge with my father. Headed for the U.P. and my first "tag along and help us track" deer hunt, I felt somewhat queasy with the knowledge that we were suspended mid-bridge and that somewhere deep in darkness both before and behind us lay terra firma and safety. Now, on another first hunt and in a solo canoe, I am visited by a similar realization. I don't get queasy this time, for I have learned to trust in and to surrender myself to the dark night.

The half-mile trip upstream, a twenty-minute jaunt in daylight, takes the better part of an hour this time. Without a guide or spotlight, I have to sense the weeds and rely on memory to maintain my bond with the channel. On matters less ancient than that first trip across the bridge, though, memory is as fogged as my senses are at times, and the channel, the clear pathway, sometimes eludes my paddle. Against the fiberglass hull of the canoe, the weeds hiss, not in anger, more as a gentle warning, like rustling leaves that announce an approaching rain shower.

And so I meander just a bit but always seek the channel. The current here is nearly non-existent, so I don't have to worry about fighting natural forces. Beyond the glare of any cabin lights, I ship my paddle and raise my eyes to the heavens, recognizing several constellations I cannot name. A half dozen falling stars tumble closer. I claim sole ownership of the view.

That fire 'twas led me on
And shone more bright than of the midday sun
To where he waited still
It was a place where no one else could come

I recognized my place by features I had noted long ago. I couched the canoe among the cattails and nestled in its bottom. A gentle breeze rocked me to repose as I awaited.

What had initially nudged me to the riverbank and encouraged me on this journey through the dark night was the early September goose season. For several years I had both promised myself to take advantage of it and then just as easily had forgotten.

Too soon, though, the sun rose, squint-high. Only two geese had flown by and I hadn't shot. But it didn't matter.

Oh night thou was my guide
Oh night more loving than the rising sun
Oh night that joined the lover
To the beloved one
Transforming each of them into the other

I had discovered and surrendered to a new love, a new passion, an outdoors activity that produces an utter and unconditional union with nature: pre-dawn paddling on flat water.

And I had navigated the straits of the dark night, self-propelled.

Surface Details

A bout a half hour into our drive home, Maureen finally broke the silence.

"Oh, those colors are so beautiful," she said, more to herself than to anyone within hearing range.

Sensing an opening and not being one to let an opportunity pass by, I butted in on her monologue: "Too bad that I've got the best seat in the Suburban, though."

"What are you talking about?"

She was speaking to me, at least.

So I waded right in. "For me, those trees are like a pleasantly painted backdrop as I gaze at the beauty at center stage. That's you, sweetheart. The beauty."

"Oh puh-leez!"

"No kidding, dear," I pressed my case. "With the sunlight filtered just a bit by those clouds, the oranges and reds become more subdued, like a jaw breaker after you've had it in your mouth awhile. Hey! That's another one. I'm just full of similes today, aren't I?"

"You're full of something."

Obviously the charm, the correct grammar and the use of a literary term hadn't produced the desired effect.

"Tom! I'm just so embarrassed. Pretty soon, I won't be able to go anywhere. How could you?"

"How could I what?"

"The gas!"

Oh. The gas. But what's the big deal? The place I had called from was less than a ten-minute drive from our cabin. It's not like she had to recruit a search party to locate me. And it was only the first time I ran out of gas in—well, in recent memory, anyway. Plus it was the absolute first time with the Jeep. Who's to say I wasn't just testing to learn how to read the gas gauge to see when the Jeep is really empty?

"The needle blocked out the great, big *E*, Tom," she said. "That should have been a clue. Besides," she added.

Boy, she just doesn't let up. And I can't deliver too much charm sprinkled with literary expertise once she gets going like this.

"Besides, I don't care that you ran out of gas. I care about what happened at the gas station."

"Hey! The sheriff let you off with a warning. What else do you want?"

Seems I had been rattled. Seems I was steaming hot. Seems my one-track mind was set on filling the gas can, getting out of there and getting back to the Jeep. Seems that she's taking this much too personally.

"You're not the one who was accused of stealing the gas, Tom!" she politely pointed out.

Yeah. Like I would have been that stupid. There I was in a small town in northern Michigan wearing a blaze orange hunting shirt, the afterflashes of which would keep your eyes pulsating well into the night. My old orange hunting cap has sprouted whiskers, and my hair is as frayed as my cap. Plus I drive around town in a red 1968 Jeepster with a distinctive, "Historic Vehicle" license plate. Wouldn't all that make me just a tad conspicuous had I intentionally tried to drive away without paying?

"I thought you had already paid for it, Tom," Maureen huffed. She had demonstrated a similar tone of disparagement shortly after the sheriff had escorted us back to the gas station and told her to wait outside.

"I'll never be able to go there again."

She went into a sulk of epic proportions, not unlike that of Achilles in *The Iliad* (reverse simile?). Well, I can't stay awake to drive if no one will talk to me. We switched drivers.

Barely buckled up in the passenger seat, I offered an olive branch. "You want some of these cookies?"

"Just leave me alone," she said, uttering each word as if it existed in a vacuum of its own.

"Your favorite, chocolate chips," I tempted her.

"That's enough, Tom."

When Maureen says that, she means business, especially when she lowers her chin and glowers at the road ahead. So I gobbled down the rest of the cookies then shook what remained from the bag into my mouth.

"And don't think I'm going to clean up that mess for you, either," she declared.

That comment called for one of my brilliant responses. Fortunately, I thought twice and stopped myself. Instead, I scooted lower in the seat and took a nap.

About an hour later, we stopped at our favorite expressway convenience store. I dallied awhile, looking for a new snack when suddenly she shrieked, covered her face and bolted for the car.

Fearing she'd spotted a mouse, I jumped into action. No sooner had the store manager pushed me down off the counter than I bolted too—like a knight rushing to the aid of his lady, you see.

Outside the car, she started in on me again.

"Tom! I'm so humiliated. I can never go back in that store again."

"What's the problem?"

Seems that on the previous leg of the journey, I'd missed my mouth with a few morsels of choco chips. Seems they had tumbled beneath me and had migrated to the inner edge of my extreme upper rear thigh. Seems that they melted. Seems that I was wearing tan pants.

"Tom! Do you know what that looked like?"

An accurate response to that question called for creative thinking, since I couldn't spin fast enough to see the seat of my pants before it disappeared behind me. Once I understood, though, I responded with my usual charm.

"Let 'em laugh. We've got each other, babe."

"You just don't get it, do you," she said, agony rising in her tender voice, misery building in her beautiful blue eyes. "And quit trying to be charming, talking about my eyes or my voice. How you look is a reflection of me."

"What?"

"People see you and they think of me. And I can't stand to have them think that I'd allow you to go out in public like that."

"Well, in that case, you probably don't want to go see Dr. Ormsbee anymore, either. Plus you'll want to consider allowing me to switch on the bedroom light when I get dressed. Probably also want a bigger dresser so we can each have our own drawers."

"Why?" She was aghast.

Seems I had gotten dressed in the dark the other morning, as usual. Seems I was heading to an appointment with our reliable chiropractor. Seems I had to drop my trousers so he could work on my extreme lower back, as usual. Seems I had donned Maureen's underpants by mistake. Seems Doc's assistant was in the room at the time taking notes.

"Maureen lets you out in public like that?" she asked.

Not any more.

Flyway

S ometimes I feel like a mallard duck among sandhill cranes.

Perhaps I should explain.

Barreling west across the U.P., I noticed something new along U.S. 2 near Manistique. Actually, what I saw was old, the most ancient of birds, the avian species most closely descendent from dinosaurs: sandhill cranes. New for me was seeing them in such great numbers as they *staged*, or assembled for their fall migration.

More than sixty of these living fossils congregated in the field alongside the highway. Apparently, they like to select their bunkmates before the long cold winter sets in, for several engaged in courtship behavior: in pairs they would face each other, leap into the air with outstretched wings and throw their feet forward. Others nonchalantly kept feeding, paying no heed. What a treat, especially when about a third of them decided to head south. With their "Ka-roo-o-o" call that sounds like a rusty gate, they lifted off, spun in their modified pinwheel flight and churned quasi-southward disappearing in the embrace of the gray sky.

On the ground near the foot of one crane, a familiar small green blot stood out. But I wanted to be sure. So I hauled out the binoculars and double-checked. There among the sandhill cranes, a drake mallard and his companion, a hen, also fed.

How odd. Didn't that greenhead know he doesn't belong with the others? He's a duck, for crying out loud, and they're cranes.

Obviously, the duck didn't share the same opinion about these matters; he just kept on eating. I would have waddled away. In fact, as I headed toward a campground rendezvous, I felt more and more like I had imagined the duck should have felt. Nine other men and I were scheduled to meet that afternoon, to renew and rekindle our friendships spawned by our annual pilgrimage in honor of wood-cock and grouse. During the drive, however, I entertained the notion that like the mallard, I don't belong.

Driving alone, I was responsible for making all decisions and the decision was made that Lucy my English setter and I would pause to hunt an inviting stand of aspen near Rapid River.

A wild flushing grouse pulled us deeper into the woods than we had planned, and not in a straight line. Before too long, we encountered a massive beaver pond that only served to confuse and confound us.

At this point, the customary situational panic sidled up and set its cold, bony fingers on my shoulder until I quietly but firmly removed them by insisting that I would refer all matters to my compass. It had set me straight before; it would do the same now. Within a few minutes we were back at the truck.

Continuing the road trip, I cogitated. The natural tendencies of the compass had guided me aright. Similarly, natural tendencies, instincts really, had told the duck to feed wherever he wanted no matter what the indignant passer-by might think. My instincts told me I didn't belong. Hmm ... what direction to follow? What inclination to trust?

That lesson simmered for the next couple of days, but I had difficulty putting it into practice.

At camp we shot some birds, had some talk and ate some meals, but something still gnawed at me, like jet lag in the woods. Still feeling I didn't belong, I left camp early.

Wildlife artist Jim Foote and his wife Joanne were ensconced at a northern Michigan cabin and had invited me to stop by if I could work a visit into my schedule. Often in times of confusion or malaise, I've been known to flee to the harbor of their friendship. Call it a natural tendency, an instinct, or an inclination but once again the compass directed me to the Footes.

The first afternoon there, Jim and I slipped into the woods with our dogs. Back at the cabin we all had some conversation and Joanne prepared a marvelous meal. Everything as it's supposed to be. Just as the shower that night rinsed the camp dirt away, their companionship cleansed me of a week's worth of disorientation and emotional missteps.

"Let's try to get some pictures," Jim said the next morning, hauling along his camera with his shotgun as we entered a favorite covert of his. Bagging birds, he said, would not be a priority.

And it wasn't.

In camp, we faithfully record how many birds we flush and shoot. Naturally, under such a working philosophy and the fact that boys will be boys, it's impossible to ignore the competitive juices. The quest for filling the game bag sometimes overpowers the importance of delighting in the dimension the dogs add to the hunt.

Not this time.

"I was lying in bed last night," Jim said, "and I couldn't remember any of the birds I've shot. I remember lots of misses, and the ones where you get good dog work. But I don't remember the kills."

Among the aspens, his Kate dog would point and Lucy would back. Then Lucy would pin a woodcock and Katie would drift in to honor her point. For the most part, we just watched and enjoyed.

Of the 13 woodcock and 4 grouse pointed in an hour and a half, we only shot at three woodcock. No need for more. Watching the dogs was enough.

By refocusing my attention on the simple, pure joys that had initially attracted me to bird hunting with pointing dogs, Jim had, like a trusty compass, guided me aright.

By rededicating myself to the quest for the appreciation of such experiences, I had gained the self-assurance, if not pure audacity, of a mallard who insists on chowing down where he sees fit—even if it means staring at crane ankles now and then.

Preliminary Findings

B ig doin's last week. For once I ended up finding more things than I lost. But since I had previously lost all the recovered items, I guess all I did was break even.

Longest lost was the magazine plug for my pump shotgun. Don't ask me how or why it ended up in a "catch all" basket on the hearth at our cabin. But there it was, just sitting there smiling at me while I churned through the basket in search of a functioning lighter so I could start a fire.

I needed the plug last spring, preparing as I was for a Pennsylvania turkey hunt. PA law says you have to have your shotgun plugged so it can't hold more than three shots, a provision that applies in Michigan only to migratory birds: ducks, geese and woodcock. Since I don't use my turkey gun for woodcock, I don't keep it plugged. But I must have used it when I went out that one time at the cabin for geese because there was the plug. But if I used it, why wasn't it with the gun at home instead of up north all by itself?

Needless to say, after churning through every conceivable—and concealable, I guess—hiding spot in our house two hundred miles south of where the plug lay in smug repose, I did not discover its whereabouts and had to buy a replacement.

Now I have a spare.

The next thing I found, I didn't find myself.

A couple weeks ago I lost my camera. It was a brand new, "slip into your pocket" size point-and-shoot, loaded with only its second roll of film. What's worse, that film held images of some special moments from the early part of the hunting season.

I'd last remembered using it as I enjoyed a leisurely hunt with wildlife artist Jim Foote. Once I got home and discovered it missing, I called him up north to see if he'd located it.

"I don't see anything here but I'll have Jim check the truck," said his wife Joanne.

Two more calls during the week did not bring the news I'd hoped for. So I made up my mind.

As soon as I could blow out of work on Friday, I headed north, on a line for the covert where Jim and I had been hunting. It made no sense. The pouch in which I carry the camera had been latched. But the camera was missing. No sense.

I churned through the brush for about a half hour, giving up when dusk and common sense told me I would never find it.

Totally confounded and absolutely confused by this point I had no other recourse but to list that little camera among the "perpetually lost" in my life. On I drove to visit the Footes. Jim greeted me at the door.

"Where've you been?" he asked.

"In the woods looking for my camera."

"I told Joanne that's where I figured you'd be. Just when we were finding this," he said, the camera dangling by its strap from his index finger.

Come to find out, on tilt-back chairs the empty space between the seat and foot rest is sometimes filled with a bridge of material which folds out of view when the chair is upright. Like a hammock, the material can comfortably nestle items like cans of insect repellent, wallets and palm-sized point-and-shoot cameras. How the item actually gets into the hammock while the chair is open and how it remains in place while the chair descends into the upright position is another matter, best explained by either a mechanical engineer or someone who's never lost a sock in a clothes dryer.

I was happy finding that camera, but I was ecstatic by the next find a couple days after I returned from the north country: a payroll check from two weeks earlier. Maureen was less than ecstatic. Then again, as someone who rarely loses anything, how could she share in the joy? Especially when so many forces figured into my success.

You see, with the roads all blocked by construction crews, traffic gets heavy fast, and I have to plan my route home even before I leave for work in the morning. That way, I take with me the stuff I need based on the places I'll visit on the way home. You know, mail if I'm going to the post office, clothes if I detour to the cleaner's and the checkbook if I'm headed to the bank.

Imagine my surprise when I showed up at the bank last Monday only to find I had forgotten to pack both the checkbook and my payroll check. Imagine my further surprise on Tuesday when, after forgetting and going home first, I doubled back and showed up with the book and check only to find the bank was closed.

Imagine my chagrin Wednesday evening as I attempted an early preparation for Thursday's ride home and couldn't locate my check or the book. I looked everywhere, three times: the truck, my brief case, my desk and work table in the home office, even churning through all the spots I had visited months earlier looking for the shotgun plug.

Maureen, just because it gives her pleasure to irk herself so she can rail at me, began churning through the garbage bags (seems lots of *churning* results from my ability to lose things and the efficiency with which I do so).

"I don't know why you don't just put the stuff in the 'banking' slot of your desk," she sweetly hissed.

That gave me an idea. As Maureen tore into another plastic bag, I headed back to my roll-top desk and peeked into the fourth cubby hole from the right. Just beneath the book of stamps and the credit card statement.

I was so proud of myself when I was able to announce, "Honey! Guess what I found, sweetheart? And you were right, dear. It was right in with the banking stuff."

Her nostrils flared, revealing flames that she was barely able to contain. I tried to douse them.

"So, ha-ha. I guess I did put this in the right pile after all, eh, sweetie-pie? I guess you're pretty proud of me for that. Right, honey babe? Good thing I didn't ask you to churn through that garbage bag for me, eh, kitten?"

The phrase "getting nowhere fast" had just found its poster child.

Nevertheless, I persisted: "Isn't that the way it is? Things are always in the last place you look, aren't they darling?"

I found myself sleeping in the basement that night.

Water Log

B oy! Those ducks and geese have been flying all around this morning, eh?" Maureen asks without facing me as I enter the cabin.

"Not where I was," I mutter, my waders squishing with my approach.

Then she turns.

Maureen's glare combines incredulity and resignation, as it does when I return from a trip to the grocery store brandishing another tabloid with a space alien story.

"You're not coming into the house in those clothes, are you?" Maureen asks.

For the novice, the above query constitutes a "wife question." They always end with an "are you" and they imply a directive as opposed to an inquiry.

"Why, yes, I am." I respond, clearly answering what I thought she'd asked, clearly the perpetual novice.

"Why?"

"Because I'm going hunting again and I don't want to get wet twice in one day. This way, I'll stay wet."

"Tom, that's just about the dumbest thing you've ever said," she politely advises.

"Oh yeah?"

"Yeah."

"Well," I carefully measure my words, "what's the dumbest?"

She shakes her head, closes her eyes and chants a familiar chorus: "Tom! Just look at you!"

Hey, I don't look so bad, not for someone who has spent two months anticipating, six hours getting ready and an hour and ten minutes putt-putting up the river and back, all for a total of 20 minutes of late season duck hunting. I am muddy from the soles to the knees of my waders, just wet from the knees to my waist. The part of my brown camouflage coat that hasn't gotten soaked in the river is as white as the driven snow. Actually, it is covered with driven snow, a wet, miserable, sticky coating that, once inside the warm cabin and despite Maureen's icy stare, quickly melts away. Southward. Inside the waders. My cheeks feel as if they display roses, but this is not the time to ask Maureen for my current rating on the cuteness scale.

"Are you happy now?" she asks.

"Not really."

"Have you learned your lesson?"

My brain is still too numb to figure out if I have, so while it thaws, I just stand there, grinning.

I know I learned some things, but I don't think Maureen wants to hear them. Most lessons revolved around the properties of liquids of various identities and in various quantities.

I learned there's a simple reason that high quality duck hunting gear is waterproof. I learned that I should acquire some high quality duck hunting gear. I learned that, spill-proof top notwithstanding, when juggled along with a shotgun, gear box, two dozen foam decoys and portable heater, a cup of coffee, tilted properly, can soak through to your chest and down the inside of your waders as you head from cabin to boat. Likewise, cold swamp juice will run downhill and silently seep over the top of your waders as your ample weight squeezes the liquid from the soft riverbank where you take a quick nap.

Long before that lesson, I found out that gasoline stored for three years in a garage won't easily ignite. But it will cause lots of heat as you grunt and sputter while attempting to pull-start an outboard motor which has sat unused for an equal amount of time.

And, spill-proof top notwithstanding, when carelessly balanced between your knees on your run for fresh gas, a cup of coffee will warm your seat while at the same time it stains the truck's gray upholstery. If you've dropped your wet waders below your knees to protect that seat while you drive, the coffee might even find its way down to warm your socks.

I learned that a 12-foot aluminum boat will handle better and gear won't float around if you replace the transom plug you had removed three years earlier to prevent water from building up while the boat was trailered. After herding the decoys back to the craft, I also gained an appreciation for the difficulty of climbing into the boat when alone and wearing waders in which the water has risen above the ankles. I also learned that water slopped aboard combines with melting snow and slush from oars and a punt pole, a gas and oil mixture leaking from an old motor's fuel line and spilled coffee to create an interesting brew which sloshes along the floor of the boat then runs up your sleeve when you tumble in from gathering decoys.

I learned that a wet, sticky snow needs only 15 minutes to whitewash all the dead-grass brown camouflage you are wearing or have brought along in the boat. It also dims the realism factor as it accumulates on the gently bobbing foam decoys, all the while encouraging real ducks to remain in the protected bays where people feed them.

Maureen tries to make some sense of it all. "Tom. Listen to me: Did anything go right out there?"

"Well, the decoys worked pretty good, I think."

But what do I know? I was waiting for ducks which abandoned the neighborhood as soon as they heard me cracking, stumbling and sloshing through the shelf ice and muck. But the season was slipping away and I needed to get in some hunting time.

I had seen in a magazine where a manufacturer had been looking for waterfowlers to field test its new models of foam decoys. After purchasing a set of decoys, you earn bonus points for every hour you log while using them under actual hunting conditions. So I volunteered.

"But you couldn't have been hunting for more than a half hour, could you?" Maureen asks. "What can you earn for that?"

"Well, actually, it was only 20 minutes of hunting. But I figure the boat ride down and back counts as realistic conditions, right? I mean, you've got to allow for travel time to and from the hunting area. So that's a total of an hour and a half. After two hours, I earn an official 'Field Tester' arm band for my hunting jacket."

"That kind of defeats the purpose of the camouflage, doesn't it?"

Boy, if I didn't know any better, I'd call that a wife question. I parry with an insightful response: "Huh?"

"So what are you going to do now, Einstein?" she asks.

"Well, maybe I won't go back out. Maybe I'll just sit here with you and watch the ducks fly by."

"Good idea," she says.

"First," I say, squishing into the kitchen, "let me get a refill of coffee."

"No!" she shrieks and dashes, just in time to witness the spill.

Two Beaners, Not to Be

T om!" Maureen called from the bedroom we use as an office. "What's the score?"

I fumbled with the remote and found the game. Lucky for me the graphic covered the screen.

"Dallas 13, Pittsburgh nuttin', honey," I cheerfully answered. Then I switched from the Super Bowl back to my show.

"That's not good enough," she said, and before I could react to her footsteps, she had entered the living room. She went into her worry dance in front of the TV screen.

"The spread is 13 1/2. I thought the Cowboys were a mortal lock on this one. I'm startin' to worry, Tom."

She continued pacing, looking at neither me nor the screen. But she also was blocking the path of the infrared signal from the remote. I was stuck in no-man's land.

"You know," she continued, "I bet my lungs this time. I won't even be able to afford the juice if Tuna man makes me pay up right away. That's what I get for chasin' that dough I laid down on the Lions to make it to the—what in heaven's name do you have on?"

Apparently, she finally saw the TV.

"Kurt Browning. He's doing some nice things on ice with his guest stars," I responded helpfully.

"You're watching a figure skating show instead of the Super Bowl?" she asked. "Why?"

"Well, I didn't see all of it the first time it aired, so I figured this was another chance."

"What has gotten into you?" she gasped.

"I'm starting to mature."

"No way. You're just getting old."

"Whaddya' mean?"

"Well, Tom, you're watching re-runs of a figure skating show during the Super Bowl. Old guys watch figure skating."

"No way! I was just channel surfing during a commercial when— Wow! Look at that Josie Chouniard. Is she graceful, or what?"

"Say, Tom," Maureen nudged as she grabbed the remote. "Can you name the Dallas Cowboy who also plays professional base-ball?"

"Uh ... uh ... well, is it Nolan Ryan?"

"Tom! You are getting old. You know more about women figure skaters than about football."

I protested her call: "That just shows I'm maturing in my sensitiv-ity. You know, as men mature, they no longer view life as a compe-tition and feel less of a need to dominate the situation. They learn to lose with grace. And that's me."

"Hah! Tell that to all the guys whose hands you refused to shake after you lost in basketball."

"That was before I started to mature."

"You mean, 'before I retired,' don't you?"

Speaking of semantics, the word *losing* can have a meaning other than not winning. It can mean no longer having and on that front, I haven't been able to mellow, either. Maureen and I are getting ready to move, a prospect which helped to clarify that realization.

"Tom!" Maureen called a couple weeks ago while I was supposed to be cleaning out my closet. "You get to work and quit lingering over stuff. I don't want to hear any more sighs or whining."

Well, it wasn't my fault I came across the repair bills for my old Grousemobile. There they were, wrapped in that pretty pink ribbon, just as I had left them, having forsaken her for a ratty, black pickup truck. I have trouble, now, whenever I think of that 1984 Ford Bronco II. Excuse me for a moment. ...

There. That's better. Let's see, what else is here?

Good news! The flashlight I thought I had lost when it fell off my desk and rolled away wasn't lost at all. It had just rolled in the direction opposite of where I looked.

Hey, here's that five dollar bill to remind me to include a suggestion in one of my columns. A hunting buddy once told me that you can prevent your shooting glasses from fogging by wiping them with a dollar bill. Something about the oils in the paper, or something. I didn't have a single on me at the time, so I tried a fiver. It turned in a pretty good job. And like Maureen always says, "For a few dollars more, you can go first class."

As you can see, finding things is more comforting than losing them.

Now in the basement, I finally locate my Bean Maine Hunting Boots—leather on top with rubber soles—which I wore only three days ago but which had mysteriously disappeared. Some sneaky Pete had stashed them in my gear closet near the rest of my boots. Oh well, just goes to show you: things are always in the last place you look.

Look and search as I do, though, I find that my other Beans—the slip-on version—are nowhere to be found. Talk about a loss. I'm almost positive I had them when my pal John Northrup and I took our steelhead trip to the Pere Marquette River a couple years ago.

We should have smelled trouble when a miscue resulted in our hooking up with a guide who is more familiar with the Au Sable River. We should have recognized difficulty when he proclaimed, "The client is always right," then enjoyed a day of contradicting our desires and requests at every bend in the river. I should have known better when he pronounced himself an authority on bird watching then admitted he'd never seen the spring mating dance of the American woodcock. Good ol' hindsight.

I remember tossing the Beaners into the back of his pickup that morning after donning my waders. I last remember rushing from the pickup to John's Explorer that night, flipping in our gear and slipping into a pair of sneakers for the ride home, away from that guide.

I must have forgotten the boots.

The guide never called.

It doesn't matter that 11 other pairs of boots are corralled in the pen. The pair I lack is the pair I seek.

Gee, I think I know how the Good Shepherd felt.

And, as I am quick to remind Maureen, he was a mature shepherd, not an old one.

Scrambled Signals

APRIL 1996

While it might come as quite a surprise to many of you, I spend a lot of my non-outdoor time pursuing matters intellectual. Oh, yes indeed. Consider my recent activities.

Astronomy: I awaken after midnight and try to convince Maureen to accompany me to the roof of our house where we can engage in some once-in-a-lifetime comet observation. She playfully taps me and mumbles something which I interpret to mean, "That's so kind of you to think of me, dear, but I just don't think the viewing conditions will be as superb as you suggest. Check with me again sometime in the next millennium."

Physics: I decide to remain in bed, not wanting to hoard all the comet viewing gusto to myself. I roll over, gingerly, and ponder the kinetic energy and dynamics which allowed her to develop such force with only an eight-inch acceleration distance before her elbow reached my ribs.

Audiology: "What are you doing in there?" Maureen will sometimes call in the afternoon when I disappear into the bedroom with Maggie our English setter.

"Pondering with Maggie."

"Which one of you two is snoring?" she asks.

"Must be Maggie because I'm pondering so deeply I wouldn't even be able to hear myself snore."

Linguistics: Sooner or later, I pull into this station and ask, am I the only man in the world whose wife, though born and raised in the same region of the same country, speaks an entirely different language?

For example, last summer, during a drive home from the cabin, she started with, "Tom, I love you."

"I love you, too, Mo."

"No, I really love you."

"And I really love you."

"You don't understand how much I love you. You know, like if you were to die I'd just be heartbroken. I wouldn't want to go on."

"Cool," I said and returned to pondering about—well, I forget what it was but you can bet it was something intellectual.

After a momentary silence, she continued.

"What about you? If I were to die, who would you leave all your stuff to?"

"My second wife, I guess," I said without too much deliberation.

At the very least, I think she expected a longer pause. And this time her elbow had twice the distance to build its momentum and the force with which the blow was delivered.

Sometimes, I've learned through patient study, she wants no answer. Like when she asks a "wife question." A wife question isn't a question at all; it's a directive against acting in a certain way. And it carries a built in warning because it always ends with, "are you?"

For example: "You aren't going to wear that shirt in public, are you?"

"Why yes, I thought I'd just"—Wham! She wasn't inquiring about my intentions. She was ordering me to change my shirt.

"You aren't going to drink right out of the milk bottle, are you?"

"Why not? It beats dirtying up another glass. Plus, nobody's coming to visit."

Wham!

'Nuff said.

And I can't begin to count the number of times she's asked, "Are these pants dirty?"

I don't get it. She knows I usually only wear clothes for three or four days between washings. Not days in a row, for I always allow stuff at least a 24-hour airing out interval. And I'm very careful about keeping them clean. Recently, I patiently explained this to her.

"Tom! You idiot! When I ask if they're dirty, I'm really asking if they're all stinky!"

Geez, you'd think she would have just said so. So now why does she throw a fit each time she asks if my pants are dirty and I bury my snoot in them and take a good whiff—all for the sake of answering her question clearly?

And just the other day while I was seeing her off at the airport, I noticed that the power walkway, the thing that works like a flat escalator, started up once someone got on it.

"I think you need to walk on it before it moves," I offered, after pondering the mechanics and electronics a while.

"Right. And the longer you walk the farther it takes you," she said. "You think if you move your feet faster it'll speed away like Fred Flintstone's car?"

Hey, now that is really a question worth pondering but she didn't wait for a response.

Then, upon her return at the end of the weekend, she scrutinized the garbage can and found two empty pizza cartons. She also painstakingly examined the refrigerator door until she could pronounce that the prints had been left by cheese curl-coated fingers.

"Tom, what did I tell you about your diet?"

"You said to 'eat good,' so I enjoyed myself."

"No, I said to eat *well*."

These linguistic problems have come to a head recently with our impending move to another house. Usually on the Saturday between our birthdays we take each other shopping for our gifts. I was pleasantly surprised a few weeks ago when Maureen announced she would drive and I was further excited as she embarked upon some pondering of her own.

"I'm not sure what to get, Tom. A side by side or an over and under. What do you think?"

I think WOW! Finally, she is going to get involved with bird hunting and will become my hunting buddy and we'll share so much time outdoors and, YES!

So I responded, "Well, I prefer the over and under shotgun with its single sighting plane. But a classic side by side shotgun is nothing to shake a stick at. I agree. Go with the side by side. By all means. That way we can trade back and forth."

She fixed me with a puzzled gaze which I mirrored as she parked in front of the appliance store at the opposite end of the mall from the sporting goods.

"I think I'll get the side by side so I can have one of those freezers with the ice cube dispenser and cold water spout on the outside, built into the door."

And don't even ask me what visions of loveliness danced in my head when she said, "Now for your present," and started musing over the merits of an automatic vs. a stick shift. Moments later we stood in a furniture store picking out a recliner chair.

Such lapses in her clear communication have attended us from the outset of this moving project. After first viewing the new house, I asked Maureen what she thought.

"Tom, it's so beautiful, but we'll never be able to afford what they're asking."

So off I went to ponder something.

A few days later she cornered me: "Did you call Bud back and make him a counter-offer?"

"I thought you said we couldn't afford that house."

"Tom! You just don't listen to me."

As moving day looms closer and closer, I myself am grousing with anxiety: "The new address has too many numbers!"

"Tom, it only has five digits. Right now we have four."

"But I'll never remember. Plus, how will I ever learn which switches work which lights?"

"You'll learn."

"And what about my canoes? Where will I keep them?"

"You'll find a place."

"That new house is so big, I won't have all my stuff jammed together in that one, tiny closet. I'll have to find all new places to store my gear. How will I ever pack for trips without forgetting stuff?"

"You'll work out a new system. Besides you forget stuff all the time."

"Yeah, but at least now I know where to look for it when I get home and want to check to see if I really forgot it or if I packed it someplace and forgot."

"Tom, you are absolutely impossible. I don't know why I ever married you."

What do you think she means by that?

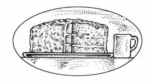

Generations

AUGUST 1996

O nce again, nature has demonstrated its ability to overwhelm the casual observer at every turn.

The recent observations to inspire this thought took place during a visit from Uncle Ray, my late father's brother, and his bride Germaine. The had flown up from South Carolina to spend their 40th anniversary with Maureen and me.

World traveler though she might be, Germaine, a southerner all her life, had never visited the Upper Peninsula. As we huddled around a map to plan our attack, she noticed the proximity of Niagara Falls and revealed that she had never seen them, either. This wonder of the world, closer than Marquette, murmured "side trip." We surrendered our itinerary to its call.

Now, certainly it boggles the mind to try to imagine just how much electricity the Falls generate, how many gallons of water spill over its escarpment per minute, how far the Falls have retreated since man first beheld them. But this time out the spectacular Falls placed second in the "defying comprehension" category. The real current that swept me away was much more subtle and came from a tiny dynamo about 150 miles closer to home.

On the way to the Falls, we stopped off to visit Ray's Aunt Cora in Port Crewe, Ontario. A bustling, self-sufficient farm and commercial fishery once perched here on the cliffs overlooking Lake Erie. My father, uncles and aunts spent parts of their summers here as children. Once grown and with children of their own, they selected Port Crewe as the site of our family reunions.

On this trip, although we cheated and used a map to be sure, the once majestic, three-story white farm house told us in no uncertain terms we had arrived.

"What do you want?" Aunt Cora crowed once Ray's knocking had finally gotten through to her one good ear. She wasn't crabby, just tired, old and uncertain. She peered from the small kitchen window, one eye blind, the other, fading.

Once Ray convinced her of who he was, she sized him up and recollected, "You didn't come to my birthday party." Last December Aunt Cora turned 100.

The big farm house still looked the same. Smelled the same, too, of old wood and natural gas from the nearby well. For the most part Aunt Cora looked the same. She was always a tiny woman but I never realized to what degree until I hugged her. With the heels of my palms on the outer edges of her shoulders my fingers nearly met in the middle of her back. She wore the same outfit in which we'd always seen her: house dress, sweater, plain black sensible shoes and those thick, old lady nylons, "Lisle" stockings Germaine called them.

When she let us in, her hair was still in the rollers the visiting nurse had installed earlier that morning. A bright fuchsia net covered her head. And while Ray and I were outside pulling the weeds Aunt Cora had said she wished someone would remove from her flower garden, Germaine removed the rollers and combed out her hair.

Incredible! Her hundred-year-old mane was as thick as could be, all brown with only a few strands of blond and white. She was widowed over 78 years ago yet she still wore her wedding ring. Her fingernails were polished. And as Germaine toiled, Aunt Cora used those gnarled, polished fingers to methodically plug the rollers plus their pins back into the thin, clear plastic cube that holds them. At one point Germaine stuck one in and, dissatisfied with the effort, Aunt Cora simply removed and replaced it according to her own specifications. She approached this task intensely like a child laboring over a round-hole, square-peg puzzle. Next, she wrapped the hair net around the cube where it would await its next assignment.

"I can't feed you," she said with the effort mustered by lungs that can't quite gather enough air. But we hadn't come to be fed. Her own lunch, some kind of a packaged meal, was warming in the stacked pans she had jerry-rigged into a double boiler.

We sat around the kitchen table to talk. In the center of the table lay a bunion pad, an adhesive bandage, some clear nail polish and a pad and pen.

"There's a Band-Aid if you need one," she indicated, then began fiddling with her hearing aid, unsuccessfully trying to reinstall its tiny battery until I intervened.

In a way, nothing's changed. Each night, Aunt Cora still ascends the old staircase to her second-story bedroom. She maintains the basement as always, neat as a pin with a place for everything. And she lives alone, the last vestige of a once thriving farm, business, household and family.

I excuse myself and visit the cliff, down whose rickety steps as children we used to scramble to get to the pier and the lake. Along the way, I notice the farm buildings have collapsed. The stepway has collapsed. Though ancient even back then, this stepway, I always thought, would endure to tempt and tease and defy me forever.

So too, the dock. All that remains is the skeleton. The rest—collapsed, disintegrated, rinsed from the shore.

I feel dented by such reminders of the inexorable passage of time. Everything has changed and I wonder if her spirit has likewise diminished.

She's so frail, so delicately mortal. Her voice is weak; her sentences come only with effort, short utterances she heaves without enthusiasm. Her visage portrays a fatigue, as if the muscles of her brow and bottom lids plead, "We've done our job on this earth; just let us call it a day and punch out." Her skin is so thin, her veins so tiny they look like blue threads beneath a layer of diaphanous wax. Her body is so ancient. It boggles the mind to imagine the amount of energy she still generates, how much of a life force her diminished blood flow transports, how far her consciousness has retreated from full awareness.

Before we depart, we ask if Aunt Cora wants us to do anything.

"Put that chair back by the window."

"Like this?" I ask.

"No. Turn it around."

"Like this?"

"No. Turn it again."

"Like this?" I give it another quarter turn.

"That's right. I have to be able to keep an eye on my neighbors."

That thought pleases her for I catch the trace of a smile. And I detect the notion of a glimmer from her good eye, a light, if not a flare.

Perhaps a flair for life persists.

Incidental Contacts

SEPTEMBER 1996

As summer quickly drifts downstream of us, I thought I'd note a few run-ins I had with nature recently.

Run-ins might not be the appropriate term for it suggests negative experiences. Let's just call them "chance occurrences" which have anchored themselves in the harbor of vivid memories.

Early on during turkey season, my pal Ray Jennings from Pennsylvania and I floated the Au Sable River in hopes of hearing some lust-crazed gobblers spout off for their girlfriends. Daylight, yawning itself awake, revealed a thick fog which hung like a barely short curtain just above the river's surface.

From the riverbank came an eerie sound, like a buzzing bee only louder. I steered the canoe toward the sound and peered towards the dimly lit bank. There, in what could best be described as a small grotto created by a spring, a hummingbird hovered, taking a drink. The hollow of wet earth amplified the wing beats and the bird sounded three times his size, like a really B-I-G bird.

The next day while hunting on foot 50 miles from that spot, we noticed movement on the path ahead of us. A tiny fawn, no more than two weeks old and all legs and spots, toddled along and kept his distance.

"His momma must be in the brush there," said Ray. "There's no way she'd leave him on his own at such a young age."

We followed quickly yet quietly on the path in single file, freezing in position each time the fawn looked back to check on us. Then Ray started bleating like a deer. This roused the fawn's curiosity and it allowed us to approach to about 10 yards. But that was the extent of the proximity it would grant us. Its tiny tail flicked like a grown-up's and the tiny deer charged ahead into the tall grass as quickly as its uncertain legs could make tracks.

About a month later, a bear cub sat atop a rise along the Trans-Canada Highway like an old man on his porch, just as pleased as punch to be watching the traffic go by.

A few minutes later, a calf moose gamboled down the middle of the road, bringing us to a halt until it decided, "This is close enough," and chose an angle leading from the pavement. More comic was its mother who watched from a curve in the road about 50 yards beyond. She was so intent on surveying our activity that she didn't even hear the red pick-up until it rounded the bend and slammed on its breaks.

"Yeow!" I think she said as she spooked, slipped on the pavement, attempted to regain a modicum of dignity then hurried after her offspring.

"Catching nature off-guard," I like to designate moments like that. And with nobody hurt it was OK to laugh about the scene.

At our cabin not long thereafter, I watched a hen mallard on the pond. Through the telescope, I could almost count the water beads on her back as she tried to nestle in for a good night's sleep. Like the cow moose, the mallard was a little off-guard. You could see her ease into her sleep mode, her head drifting back ever so slowly until her bill was just about tucked into its resting position along her back.

Then came the barking from a dog in someone's yard. You could tell when the sound waves reached the duck a beat and a half later, for up popped her head and she snapped once again to full attention. This happened several times until one of us got too tired of watching and did some easing into the sleep mode of his own.

Back home one morning, Maureen was treated to a chance occurrence of her own, though she would probably tell you it was more like a close encounter of the unwanted kind.

We take our morning walk in the darkness before the August heat and humidity seize the day. A portion of our route, perhaps 75 yards of it, passes an undeveloped, overgrown plot of land. Critters live there. Some are active in the dark. Especially skunks.

"Oh, no!" she enunciated too clearly for comfort and she froze in place two steps in front of me.

"What?" I asked, looking past her shoulder and not liking what I saw.

The outline of a skunk had stepped onto the sidewalk not three yards in front of us and had begun walking in the same direction, away from us. But luck was with us. At the sound of Maureen's voice, the skunk turned back toward us to check out the commotion. It recognized us as interlopers but had to spin around again to get his business end pointed in our direction.

In a flash (as flashy as an overweight, gimpy, tired ex-jock can be) I snatched Maureen by the armpits and began hauling us backwards. Her feet churned like a cartoon character's as he winds up to make a get-away. We retreated for about 20 yards then resumed our course, taking the road this time and giving our friend a wide berth. As we passed, we smelled concrete evidence that the skunk's business end had been properly loaded and primed and had fired.

"Cool, Mo," I chattered a quarter mile later as we returned to the sidewalk. "I've never known anyone to get that close to a skunk without getting bathed in a green mist. Yessir, you just did something unique."

Maureen, however, was less than impressed with the part she had played as a footnote in natural history.

"You go first next time," she decreed.

Ain't gonna' happen.

Endangered Species

SEPTEMBER 1996

M rr-eee-ee!"

Unsure if I had heard things correctly, I just kept on painting the new wooden fence our backyard neighbor had thoughtfully installed. But through the "whump-whump" of the roller's passing over the wooden slats, the sound persisted:

"Mrr-eee-ee!"

Squinting past the low branches of the spruce tree, my nearsighted eyes thought they recognized a pair of human legs behind the chain link fence along the side of our lot. So I moved two steps closer for confirmation.

The tiny woman leaned on the fence, stood on her toes and called once more with all the strength she could muster: "Maur-eee-een!"

After a five-month battle with a lung infection requiring two hospital stays and major surgery, Sharon isn't yet capable of holding enough air to be able to bellow and enunciate at the same time.

"Hey, Sharon," I said as I approached.

"You're not Maureen," she observed.

"That's why they call me 'Tom,'" I offered. I'm pretty helpful that way.

"Bud will never believe this. Bud!" she called. Maybe he has better hearing than I do. Maybe it's because his name is only one syllable. Perhaps he's just better trained. But Sharon's husband responded to the first call.

"What do you want, Sharon?" he asked, then noticed me as he approached. "Hello, Thomas."

"Hey, Budman."

"I was wrong," Sharon informed Bud. "It was Tom out there, not Maureen." Turning back she half-accused me, "What's wrong with Maureen?"

"Nothing, why?"

"She's such a hard worker. She's always out here doing things. Every day as soon as she gets home from work she's out here digging, raking, adjusting her sprinklers, mowing her lawn. Before work, too. But I never see you out here, except when you're loading your truck for a trip. Or when you take a break from working on your column."

Ah, the column. Time for a little prayer of thanksgiving two months early. Because somehow I might have led them to believe that I spend about six hours a day plus my entire weekends crafting these wonderful little chunks of literature. If I couldn't use the name of the column in vain, I could not justify my usual habit of ignoring yard work, not in their eyes, anyway.

And Sharon is perplexed because she's not used to seeing a man who is perfectly willing to let his wife deal with the weeds and the pine needles and earwigs. Earwigs are those pinching bugs ol' Ricardo Montalban tortured people with in that one Star Trek movie, *The Wrath of Khan*, and they give me the creeps and bite me and make my fingers swell up but they leave Maureen alone so why shouldn't she do the work out there? Besides, Maureen doesn't have to produce a column every week.

No, Sharon is used to a man like Bud with whom she has spent the 40 years of her adult life. Bud, general manager of a landscaping firm, is the kind of guy who on Friday of Labor Day weekend says, "Boy, am I glad to be away from work for three days." Then he builds a berm and a rock wall in front of his new house, plants a tree whose dirt ball weighs in at six hundred pounds, replants two dozen bushes, helps Maureen close down our swimming pool, relocates a sprinkler head, paints a trellis, tapers the yard from the driveway's edge with topsoil and lays 50 yards of sod. Sunday and Monday he gets down to some serious business. It made me tired just to watch from my office window. Working on the column, you see.

I have to be careful, for any yard work I undertake does pose a threat to my excellent record for meeting deadlines.

Why, the reaching and arm-sweeping involved in painting the fence is similar to that required when washing the Suburban, movements I abandoned long ago because they throw out my back. Also make my arms tired. Hard to hold them above my waist. Tough to type in anything but sentence fragments.

Smacked my right index finger with a rubber mallet while replacing a sprinkler head after accidentally cutting through the water supply line with a shovel. Should have known better than to attempt such a highly technical move. Momentary lapse as I tried to smoothe out the driveway edge like Bud had. Right index finger throbbed for a week; perceptive readers of the column back then would have noticed a dearth of words which required the letters j, y, u, h, n or m.

Next, I encountered the splitting maul.

During a log splitting maneuver at the cabin, every now and then a tough piece of oak defied me and insisted I drive the maul through with a sledge hammer. To accomplish this, I'd have to steady the maul by grasping its handle with my right hand and deliver the blow with the sledge in my left. To my surprise and eventual distress, one log surrendered after only one of my apparently mighty whacks. But the maul continued on its path, swinging like a pendulum. Until it met my shin. This action transpired the day before the opening of bird hunting season and threatened my ability to gather story material. It also allowed me to break my personal record for profanities spouted per second as I danced around that split oak like a druid in fast forward.

Additionally at the cabin, Maureen has relieved me of any fire building responsibilities since I burned my trigger finger (the same one as I whacked with the mallet, come to think of it) while attempting to add a log to the fire without hurting my back or grazing my shin. So even if I had been able to walk gracefully through the woods on opening day, I still wouldn't have been able to shoot at anything.

As I basked in the glow of Sharon and Bud's admiration, a voice came from behind the swimming pool. "Hey! What's goin' on over there?" Maureen called as she stood up and approached us.

"Where were you?" Sharon asked.

"Down there, painting the base of the fence," Maureen explained.

"What!" Sharon huffed as much air as she could gather. "The base is the tough part of the painting. Even Tom could have figured that out. Why couldn't he paint that part?"

Uh-oh.

Time to work on the column. Tired arms notwithstanding.

Oh, October!

*W*ell, *it's a marvelous night for a moondance*
With the stars up above in your eyes
A fantabulous night to make romance
'Neath the cover of October skies

That's according to Irish singer Van Morrison in his popular song, "Moondance."

That tune makes me want to find room somewhere in its lyrics for the sentiment, "Oh, October!" What I really mean is "The *O* of October," the full circle of fall, the hunter's moon. Not just the words which identify this wonderful phenomenon but also those which convey both the meaning it's held for mankind through the ages and the spell it's cast over me.

The hunter's moon plays itself out as only a slightly less spectacular version of the harvest moon from the previous month.

Long about September 21 or so at the autumnal equinox, the sun rises almost exactly east and sets directly in the west. The harvest moon is the full moon which occurs just before the equinox. The moon rises opposite the sun. The two team up, illuminating the sky from both sides and affording farmers about an hour more of a soft twilight by which they can harvest their crops.

The hunter's moon likewise provides hunters some extra light as they traverse the fields near day's end. Kind of like a blessing from the gods of the hunt.

Actually, it probably should be called a blessing from the goddess. Artemis, Greek goddess of the moon (amended to "Diana" by the Romans), was also in charge of hunting and wild things. If she smiled upon them, Greeks believed, they would enjoy a successful hunt.

This pale-glowing autumnal orb, October's spotlight rising slowly in the eastern sky, this hunter's moon inspires more than poetry this time of year. More than one wife has snuggled in the arms of her husband 'neath its romantic glow, warmed to the brim with his loving gazes first at her then to the sky. Until he pipes up, "That's a woodcock moon. Hunting should be good tomorrow."

Popular hunting lore as well as some scientific speculation holds that full moon nights encourage woodcock to move, ostensibly because the north/south running roads and river bottoms of their migration routes show up better in the light. Last week, the night before the scheduled appearance of the hunter's moon, the clear sky revealed one nearly full, enough for a moondance, enough for a woodcock migration. I slept, consorting with dreams of feathered phantoms who would stop over on their journey south and haunt some mutually appealing coverts.

The next morning, unwilling to let the day get much of a jump on us, Lucy and I hit the woods not long after first light. We visited the locale of our most recent covert action, allured by the thoughts that the spot is a natural rest area for birds heading south and that last night's moon should have encouraged them to do a little traveling.

There are times when you just wish someone else had been present, both as witness and as co-star sharing the sweet nectar into which you've so pleasantly and unexpectedly tapped. Yet the sweet drink's enchantment comes from the knowledge that it's yours alone to savor.

Saturday was such a day.

As soon as I said it—and I mean the exact moment I told Lucy, "Go find some birds," while I uncased my gun and locked the Jeep—she zipped directly to a spot about 40 yards away and locked up on point. That woodcock escaped without my firing even a warning shot. But only a few moments later, Lucy pinned another.

Then another.

Soon, I was passing up shots just because there was no need to poke wildly at birds I could only glimpse. Passing up those I kicked up myself on my way to find her on point. Absolving myself for poor shooting on the potential woodcock double because this was turning into a day of almost boundless opportunity.

We reached an open spot where we have to cross a swale. Lucy dashed ahead, jumped into the thick spruce and aspen cover and leaned into another point, waiting for me to catch up. The grouse entertained no such courtesies and launched itself on a freedom flight before I got more than two steps into the thickness.

Soon I realized that the grouse we were finding near the low-hanging spruce boughs were not going to fly very high; if I wanted a clean shot, I'd have to drop to their level. So when each of the next two flew, I quickly squatted while mounting the gun to my shoulder and my shooting percentage on grouse began to soar.

So went the morning. Though it's barely larger than an acre, Lucy and I drifted through the cover three times and still didn't hunt all of it. I'd start to head in one direction but some irresistible scent would draw her away. I'd dutifully follow and be rewarded with several more flushes.

Now, this has never happened before and most likely will never happen again, but we had to return to the car because the weight of the game bag began to strain my back. No lie. In only two hours. Seemed like a fine time to take a break.

The picture of contentment, Lucy and I smiled away as we shared a couple of hunter's sausages from the party store along the route back to the cabin. Then we rested.

When afternoon arrived, I should have been thinking about heading back into the woods. After all, I was only a few birds short of my limit for both grouse and woodcock.

But the morning had gone so perfectly, I didn't want to risk a bad hunt in the afternoon. On the other hand, how often does a hunter get the chance to be afield on a Saturday when the hunter's moon begins to rise? But even though I needed a few more birds to have enough for an upcoming dinner, I felt no need to shoot again that day. Then again, we still wanted a few more birds for that dinner.

This vacillation evaporated with the re-emergence of this re-minder: in the mind of ancient man, the hunter's moon represented a divine consecration of the hunt.

Mine had already been sanctified.

From my dock that night, I watched the moon rise.

From my bed I savored its blessings.

Moment of Truth

NOVEMBER 1996

The snow squall punched its way over the hill and across the hollow like a boxer doing his roadwork. It hissed like campfire embers shaken to attention by the dregs of a coffee cup. Just over the hill, darkness pawed and snorted, anxious to be freed from its stable and to overtake the day.

Bud looked to me for direction, guidance. He could tell from the change in my demeanor that things had become serious.

"This is the one situation in which all grouse hunters fear to find themselves," I cautioned.

Since Maureen and I moved into our new house, I've learned many things, most of which I never desired to know and have even less desire to act upon. Things like, thanks to the sprinkler system, the rapid pace at which a regularly watered lawn will grow. Or the increase in home heating bills when the home you are heating is twice as big as the home you used to heat. Stuff like that. A pleasant note, though, has been my new bud, Bud, our next door neighbor.

I've learned from Bud, too. I've learned that keeping pace with Bud means choking up on your shovel so you can dig faster. Keeping pace with Bud, I've learned, means working outdoors until dark and starting at first light on weekends. Keeping pace with Bud means buying work boots for the yard because your old basketball shoes just can't handle the abuse. Keeping pace means carrying both a slotted and a Phillips head screwdriver in the back pocket of your jeans just in case you pass some loose screws on your way to or from another task. It means thinking nothing of planting 300 stems of ground cover, all in the name of a couple hours' worth of work after dinner. In short, I've learned there's no keeping pace with Bud.

So I plotted: If one cannot outpace Bud, one must corrupt him.

I sowed the seeds by offering some extra shotgun shells I had "found" after our move. Then an extra pair of hunting pants. An orange cap. Some teasing words now and then about how wonderful my English setter Lucy would hunt and the allure of Maureen's gleaming presence as hostess. By mid-summer I had elicited a promise that he and his wife Sharon would visit our cabin during bird season.

How could he resist? Decades had elapsed since he last uncased his father's old shotgun. Plus, Sharon always says he works too hard and needs to learn to play. Might as well learn from the master.

Preliminary field notes were issued not long after we hit the woods.

"Head at an angle toward the dog," I directed Bud, for Lucy quickly went on point. "But keep going. Walk right past her. These grouse will run."

"OK," he said. "You're the expert."

Hey, he learns fast!

The grouse that weekend did run. And they flew, from far, far away. Sometimes we weren't even sure if we had heard birds flush. I saw one escape from the top of a 40-foot tall tree at a distance of about 70 yards. Needless to say, the birds weren't holding well for the dog.

One did, however, and Bud remembered his lesson.

Lucy chased and pointed and trailed and pointed a bird for about 300 yards. Finally, running out of cover, the bird launched itself about 30 yards in front of Bud who had just passed Lucy. His gun spoke once.

"You get it?" I called, moving in to help him search.

"I'm not sure."

After a few minutes I piped up, "I really don't think you got it 'cause I watched you shoot. You held that gun barrel absolutely still and didn't swing through the bird at all. I'd say he's still flying."

"Whatever you say," Bud agreed, and we resumed our original course.

He trusted me because I had taught him so many other important things: how to mosey through the woods, how to take an afternoon nap at the cabin between hunts and how to taunt our cholesterol levels by munching on hunter's sausage from local party stores. All the stuff he never has time for at home.

Then comes this one grouse not long before that snow squall.

I had taught Bud how grouse will never let you catch them in the open and how these late season birds would most likely be hunkered down in the overgrown valleys between oak ridges. We began to cross a desolate looking, 40-yard wide hollow populated by only a couple scrub evergreens and one pathetic oak. Lucy got hot. She pointed, reset, pointed and reset. I trotted to the right and ahead of her, Bud hustled ahead on the left.

Only one gnarled, dismal looking pine tree stood between us and the ridge. Like magic, from a stump of grass no bigger than my boot, the grouse launched itself and veered toward the scrawny boughs of that pine. Bud's gun spoke once, mine twice. The bird flew on.

"I really should have hit it," Bud said.

"No, no, Bud, that won't do," I replied, always the patient teacher, administering a final lesson.

"Well, you should have. You held that gun barrel absolutely still and didn't swing through the bird at all."

"That won't do, either," I shot back with a force and determination which someone might have foolishly mistaken for anger.

Bewildered, I added, "It was so open, I didn't even think a bird would be in there—Hey! that can be your excuse."

We had both fired, though, so we still had to agree upon an excuse for me. One which will account for two shots. That's when the snow breezed by and the fear set in. How could I talk my way out of this latest miss? I started pacing.

Revelation paid an unannounced but welcomed visit as the words occurred to me at the same moment they escaped my lips:

"I missed because ... I began swinging through the bird when it flushed while at the same time, like a good host, I waited for you to shoot. By the time you shot, I was all twisted up and couldn't swing any more."

"Good deal," Bud said. "Let's go tell Sharon."

Bud was quiet for the first several minutes on the ride back to the cabin. Then he spoke,

"You know, I think that Chauncey and Skittles need another dog for a friend. And I think it should be an English setter."

Now he's talking.

After a few more minutes of cogitation he spoke again: "You know, what? Come to think of it, I didn't really get a good look at that grouse because I lost it when it crossed the spot in my bifocals where the long distance lens meets the reading glasses."

Corruption complete.

A Dickens of a Defense

DECEMBER 1996

Once again, modern science has finally caught up to insights into the human condition offered by authors from many generations past.

The author to be highlighted this time of year: Charles Dickens. The work: *A Christmas Carol.*

The case to be made: Give Ebenezer Scrooge a break; he couldn't help being the way he was.

Granted, Scrooge was, "a squeezing, wrenching, grasping, scraping, clutching, covetous old sinner! Hard and sharp as flint, from which no steel had ever struck out generous fire; secret, and self-contained, and solitary as an oyster. The cold within him froze his old features, nipped his pointed nose, shrivelled his cheek, stiffened his gait; made his eyes red, his thin lips blue; and spoke out shrewdly in his grating voice. ... He carried his own low temperature always about with him; he iced his office in the dog-days; and didn't thaw it one degree at Christmas."

In short, he was a Scrooge all year long. Fair enough. But it's obvious that Dickens intends for us to focus on the holidays as the source both of Scrooge's afflictions and of his "reclamation," as the Ghost of Christmas Past puts it.

What's always bothered me is the fact that none of the other characters in the book—not even sappy ol' Tiny Tim—seems to understand why Scrooge is so ornery. Just look at his life and the bleak memories of the holidays he harbors in his heart. In his youth, rejected by his father, he was shunted away from his family and during the Christmas break he remained the only student at boarding school.

"A solitary child, neglected by his friends," says the Ghost of
Christmas Past.

Scrooge's earliest memories tell him Christmas is a time of
loneliness. On another Christmas Eve, his girlfriend dumped him.
On still another, while his partner Jacob Marley lay on his deathbed,
Scrooge sat at his office, "and there he sat alone. Quite alone in the
world."

No wonder the poor guy's got the holiday blues.

Fairly recent advances in mental health treatment, however, reveal
Charles Dickens to be a visionary. For there's something more to
Scrooge's sour mood than the blues. Scrooge suffers from Seasonal
Affective Disorder (SAD).

"That's certainly an interesting theory," says suburban Detroit
psychotherapist Jan Champion.

The onslaught of SAD commences in fall as the amount of
daylight dwindles. Relief comes in spring. The winter solstice,
around December 21, is the shortest day of the year and offers the
least amount of sunlight as the earth rears back and the sun darts
across the southern sky. Just in time for Christmas Eve.

The symptoms of SAD include lethargy, alteration of sleep
patterns, weight gain, a craving for carbohydrates and according to
Dr. Norman E. Rosenthal, M.D., one of the first to treat SAD in
1979, "mood disturbances severe enough to affect quality of life."
The symptoms are similar to those of clinical depression but they
subside with the return of the sun in spring.

So what about Scrooge? We can all agree he had mood disturbances, right? And being interrupted by three spirits in one night
certainly shows an alteration in sleep patterns. While Dickens
doesn't paint him as lethargic, Scrooge certainly is not energetic: all
he does is work, eat and sleep. Though he doesn't openly crave
carbohydrates, Scrooge might have been indulging, for he tries to
excuse the appearance of Marley's Ghost as, among other things, "a
fragment of an underdone potato."

Says Champion, "He certainly suffered from some sort of condition and SAD is plausible."

She further explains the fact that he otherwise displayed signs of depression year round fits in with what she's experienced in her practice: "I tend to see more people with depression that is exacerbated by the dwindling light each year. I see that as a seasonal component" to an existing condition.

More conclusive evidence to support the "Scrooge is SAD" diagnosis comes from comparing results of contemporary medical research to the light/dark imagery Dickens presents throughout the book.

Studies indicate that in the northern hemisphere, SAD generally strikes people who live north of the 40th parallel where there are fewer than 10 hours of sunlight per day in December. For a reference, Steubenville, Ohio, is located just a bit north of the 40th; Detroit, the 42nd. Scrooge lives in London at the 51st parallel. In North America, this spot compares to the east coast of Newfoundland. Listen to Dickens' description of London on that second-most famous Christmas Eve in all of Christendom:

"It was cold, bleak, biting weather: foggy withal. ... The city clocks had only just gone three, but it was quite dark already: it had not been light all day."

After working all day in his dismal office, Scrooge takes "his melancholy dinner in his usual melancholy tavern." So it's obvious that Dickens is aiming for a mood of darkness, both in London and in Scrooge's spirit.

Here's the best part: Scrooge responds to treatment like any SAD patient today.

The most effective and common treatment for SAD is light therapy. Researchers expose patients to massive doses of artificial sunlight each day. The light can't come from regular light bulbs, for neither are they bright enough nor do they reproduce the broad spectrum of light rays that the sun does. A tanning booth doesn't count, for the light has to enter through the eyes to be effective. Special lamps have been developed for this purpose and a vast majority of patients respond to this treatment.

Compare this to the circumstances which bring Scrooge out of his mood. Once he's visited by Marley's Ghost and the Spirits of Christmas Past and Christmas Present, he's ready to mend his ways.

Marley's Ghost gets him started. When Scrooge sees Marley's face on the door knocker, "it was not in impenetrable shadow as the other objects in the yard were, but had a dismal light about it..."

Think back. What accompanies the next two spirits but a preternatural glow, a flame, or halo if you will. In short, a massive dose of light.

"The strangest thing about" Christmas Past, Dickens writes, "was that from the crown of its head there sprung a bright clear jet of light."

And Christmas Present was "a jolly Giant, glorious to see; who bore a glowing torch, in shape not unlike Plenty's horn, and held it up, high up, to shed its light on Scrooge."

Ah, but how does one explain the Ghost of Christmas Yet to Come? He has no light. Except for its outstretched hand, "it would have been difficult to detach its figure from the night, and separate it from the darkness by which it was surrounded."

Remember, before Scrooge draws near to the tombstone, which he's pretty sure bears his name, he wants to believe that this spirit is previewing shadows that *may* be instead of those which *will* be. He realizes he needs to change. Plus, year round Scrooge has been displaying signs of depression.

As William Styron points out in his autobiographical account, *Darkness Visible*, depression left untreated is fatal. Additionally, the 15th century Spanish mystic St. John of the Cross identifies a period of "spiritual aridity" through which one must pass in order to grow. John calls this stage of development the "dark night of the soul."

The combination of these two insights delivers an interpretation that clearly fits Scrooge. The Ghost of Christmas Yet to Come serves as a reminder that he is at a psychological crossroad. He has a choice to make and must chart the course he'll follow for the rest of his life.

And Scrooge reacts by demonstrating that the spirits have successfully passed the torch.

He awakens "glowing with good intentions."

He runs to the window, throws it open and beholds, "No fog, no mist; clear, bright, jovial stirring, cold; cold, piping for the blood to dance to; Golden sunlight; Heavenly sky; sweet fresh air; merry bells. Oh, glorious. Glorious."

He sounds like a SAD patient in spring.

"It makes sense," says Champion. "And it makes Scrooge a more sympathetic character."

Case closed.

Passing Muster

JANUARY 1997

S ee ya' later!" I proclaimed to the bed as I tromped into the bedroom.

"Where do you think you're going?" Maureen's voice materialized from an air hole in the blankets.

"Outdoors," I chirped.

"Why?"

"Because I'm an outdoors writer. And I have to go there."

"Why?"

"To find something to write about. Geez, Maureen. You wanna' get up to speed here?"

"Tom, you idiot! You'll freeze to death out there with the wind chill."

"Now, now my dear, I can handle a little frigid weather. Besides, you went out to get the newspaper."

"Yeah, and you see where I am now. It is downright nasty cold out there. Plus, the traffic reporter on the radio said not to go out unless you absolutely had to."

"I can handle a little traffic."

"It's not the cold or the traffic I'm worried about."

"What, then?"

She pushed away the blankets, sat up, looked me straight in the eye and directed, "Take off your pants."

"What?"

"Put your purse on the dresser and take your pants off."

"It's not a purse. It's an L.L. Bean Three-Way Gear Organizer and Field Companion," I corrected with precision.

"Just put it on the dresser and take off your pants."

"Cool." She knows how much I like it when she takes charge.

"Your socks, too."

I shivered there wearing my sweatshirt, boxer shorts and a goofy smile and anticipating her next command.

"Now, you want to know what I'm looking at?"

"A nice set of legs for a man?"

"No!" Maureen corrected with a precision of her own and began to point out several deep purple souvenirs I bear on my gams.

"That scar is from where you rammed into the coffee table on Thanksgiving."

"I was doing my victory dance after beating your Dad in cribbage," I tried to inject.

"I don't care. Your right heel is scarred from where you scraped it on the shower door. And your ankle is still swollen and bruised from that fall you took Christmas morning."

"Lousy carpet."

"No, Tom. What did you have to promise before you were allowed to put on the *Riverdance* video?"

"Watch, don't dance."

"And what did you do?"

"Lousy irresistible music."

She pressed on. "But you know what? The scar that really gets me is that tiny one on your left foot. Tom, you are the only person I know who can injure himself shifting in his chair while on the telephone."

"Lousy sharp edge on my wooden work table."

"The point is, Tom, you aren't going outdoors today because I can't trust you not to kill yourself."

"No way. Besides," I said, exercising absolute authority, "these were all suffered indoors."

Apparently the only authority exercised in our home is relative, not absolute. And the relative who commands all the authority spoke next.

"You're staying indoors today for some nice, safe quality time,

Tom. So get dressed and put your purse away."

For effect, I waited until hiking up my pants to announce: "I told you! It's not a purse. It's an L.L. Bean Three-Way—"

"You keep your wallet in it?"

"Yes."

"Keys?"

"Well, yeah," I said.

"Spare change, comb, pencil and paper?"

"What's your point?"

"It's a purse."

This charge called for a quick and incisive retort.

"Oh yeah?"

The desired effect of my words eluded her.

"No matter what you call it, Tom, it's still your purse."

"I bet I've got stuff in it that makes it not a purse."

"OK. Let's see."

Inside the front pocket she found a roll of electrician's tape and a few pieces of rawhide in various lengths.

"Tom, you've got broken shoelaces in there. Why?"

"Just in case. Go on. Look some more. Check out the main pocket."

"Let's see. Small camera, folding knife in a sheath, two 9-volt batteries, multi-tool in a sheath, Chapstick, Swiss Army knife, Blistex and—Tom, why are there four pairs of sunglasses in here?"

"Those aren't sunglasses; they're shooting glasses and there should only be two pairs."

"What?"

"See, there are the dark ones and the vermilion ones I always use. Jerry Dennis left the clear ones and amber ones during woodcock camp."

"Why are his glasses in your bag?"

"They aren't. I mean they're there but they're not his. They're mine. He was just borrowing them. But he didn't wear them."

"He borrowed your glasses without wearing them?"

"Yeah. They gave him a headache."

"How could he tell if he didn't wear them?"

"Huh?"

"Never mind. What's this?"

She held out a sheet of paper I'd torn from a pocket notebook. On it appeared several names: "Babe, Belle, Molly, Kate, Maeve, Pete, Jake, Keats, Blake, Banquo, Jack." A line was drawn through "Jake."

"What's this?"

"Dog names."

"Why is Jake crossed out?

"Because I gave that one to Jerry."

"What?"

"We were in woodcock camp and he said he wanted a pup if Lucy has a litter and we got to talking about good dog names. Since he wanted a male and since you said we'd never have males again, I told him I was saving the name of Jake but he could have it."

"So what you're telling me is you gave him permission to use the name, right?"

"No. I just gave him the name."

When it became apparent that I felt no further explanation was needed, she slid away from the edge of the bed where I sat and double-checked to be sure I wasn't moving any closer.

She dug deeper into my purse and soon held up three disks about the size of dimes.

"What are these and why do you have them?"

"Subway tokens. In case I ever return to Toronto."

She didn't even ask for more details this time. She merely emptied the rest of the contents of my purse on the bed.

She was puzzled by a group of similar objects that lay there amid the Ottawa National Forest map, empty film canister, wood tick remover, candy wrappers and eyeglass cleaning fluid.

"Tom, why are there eleven peanuts in here?"

"Huggler gave them to me during woodcock camp when we visited Bond Falls."

"Why?"

"To eat, I guess."

"No. Why are they still here?"

"Because I didn't eat them."

Maureen calmly replaced the items in my purse and zipped it close. She then issued her next directive.

"Why don't you go outdoors, dear?"

"Huh? Why?"

Quality time had expired.

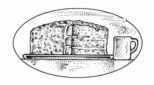

Thinking About Mr. Woodcock

FEBRUARY 1997

Maureen stepped into the office and read over my shoulder as I completed my list:

1. Can't see without squinting.
2. Stories lose their way for several minutes before heading in a direction which lacks a climax worthy of the wait.
3. Same stories get repeated with regularity.
4. Misses beneath ears when shaving.
5. Says "Beg pardon?" instead of "Pardon me?"

"Whatcha' got there, Tom," she prodded, "notes for your autobiography?"

The stern look I gave her shocked her into sensibility and I spoke up. "No. I've made a list of traits common to geezers."

"As I said," she laughed, then danced away and mumbled something.

"Beg pardon?" I asked.

"Never mind. So what is this?"

"I tried to tell you, I wrote down everything guys do when they become geezers."

"Why? Early Warning System?"

The laugh and the dance erupted once more.

"Lookit, Mo. If you don't take my work serious, then just go away."

"Seriously."

"What?"

"It's *seriously* not *serious*. I don't take your work seriously."

"Oh. OK. Thanks. I'll fix that."

"So what's the list for?"

"Well, I was thinking about Andy Ammann. I mean he's 86 years old. He's retired. He and his wife have been living in the same house for almost 40 years. You'd think he'd be acting like a geezer about now."

"But he isn't?"

"No. His eyes and hearing are fine. His stories stay focused. Plus they're interesting. He's got that bad back, you know, so he uses a pair of ski poles to help him when he walks around outside. But you don't have to be a geezer for that."

No, Dr. Andy Ammann is not a geezer. Nor is he a coot or a curmudgeon. He's a gentleman in the late autumn of his years, a retired Michigan Department of Natural Resources ornithologist. Scientist by education and profession, he nevertheless cares enough about language to use *who* and *whom* correctly.

The appellation "Mr. Woodcock" probably applies more to Andy Ammann than to anyone else in the state or the country. It is he who perfected the techniques for using pointing dogs to help with banding woodcock in the spring, thus opening the door for non-professionals to assist in the gathering of scientific data.

Andy and his wife Ellen have lived in Haslett, near Lansing, since 1958. A lifetime's worth of memories decorate the walls and perch on tables and desks. Even a songbird perches in its cage on a coffee table in the living room. Attempting to note every detail seems like prying, so this general impression must suffice.

The house is built into the side of a hill. At one end, the basement empties into the garage, one side of which nestles into the base of the slope.

Inside, a cinder block wall partitions the garage and defines Andy's workshop. The room is narrow, perhaps eight-feet wide, about twenty-feet long. Both here and upstairs, radios are tuned to a classical music station. The aria from some opera I'll never recognize fills both levels of the home.

It's here in the workshop that Andy creates mementos for up-and-coming DNR retirees. He fashions feather wreaths and other displays from the materials stored in more than 20 boxes he's labeled and shelved. Shoe boxes, old cigar boxes, flat boxes. Each marked with its special contents like "finished w/c tails." The *w/c* is short-hand for *woodcock*. Other boxes feature "buckskin ... chukar tails ... sage grouse ... ruffs (selected)" and so on.

Drying in a corner are a couple lengths of osage wood out of which Andy makes his own recurve bows. A homemade rack holds nearly two dozen arrows which have taken deer, wild turkey, fox. Once an arrow claims a victim, it is retired to the rack.

Throughout the workshop, the garage itself and Andy's basement, caps of hunter's orange dot the landscape. And his memory is similarly adorned with images of his dogs, mostly with the black flecks of English setters.

For example, consider how Andy and Ellen came to own the property in Tennessee to which, until recently, they would retreat during winter.

"On the way back from visiting our son in South Carolina, we stopped off to visit some old friends. The fella' had just lost his job and asked if I wanted to buy a portion of his land down there. I went on a walk with my two dogs and both went on point."

Andy stood near the top of a ridge while the dogs struck scent in the shallow valley.

"A grouse flushed from a tree and flew right past me."

He returned to his friend's cabin and offered to buy an acre on the spot.

When he views old 8mm films that have been transferred to video or some old segments of the *Michigan Outdoors* TV show in which he appears, he's enchanted by the work his dogs turn in.

"Oh what memories!" he chirps. Not wistful or nostalgic, though. He's more analytical and factual about what he's viewing. But the analyses clearly engender much joy.

"I don't see how anyone can say he does not want a dog that retrieves," he says as, with grouse in mouth, his old Dolly bounds into view in the age-faded film. "I wouldn't have one that doesn't."

He admits that he's been lucky enough to own setters with natural retrieving instincts, like his current dog Patches who has retrieved his keys, his granddaughter's cassette tape from a raging creek in Tennessee and his buddy's glove two weeks after it had been dropped in the woods.

"Did you ever have a dog stop in the middle of a retrieve and point another bird?" Andy asks out of nowhere.

He recounts the time his wonderful setter Kate descended a hill to retrieve a grouse and when she didn't return he walked down and found her on point with the grouse in her mouth. Another grouse flushed.

Once in South Carolina, the hunters had given up on a quail they had dropped, but Katie didn't. "Soon she came trotting up the road with it then turned onto point just like that."

He illustrates by snapping his left arm to horizontal attention, tugging on the right as if he were drawing a bow and leaning into a point of his own.

"I suspect that many quail hunters would have that happen but not so much with grouse and woodcock."

Andy got his first bird dog when he started working for the DNR in 1939.

"When I first reported to the Department, my boss, Harry Ruhl, says, 'Andy, have you got a bird dog?'

"'No.'

"'Well, you better get one.'"

Previously, Andy had earned his bachelor's and master's degrees at the University of Iowa. He took his doctorate in zoology with a minor in ornithology from the University of Michigan in 1938. Upon joining the Department, he took a job which nobody else wanted: conducting the prairie chicken and sharptail grouse studies in the Upper Peninsula.

"Harry wanted me to be the envoy in the U.P. where all they knew was riding the roads in Jeeps and shooting from the car."

"Near Seney, we'd be listening for sharptails. We'd hear the wolves start to howl. You could see the dogs were listening, too. Then they'd imitate the wolves."

Patches demonstrates once Andy throws back his head and calls, "Patch, Aooooo!"

After World War II, Andy moved to the Lansing office and began working on all game birds. His woodcock research was actually jump-started by efforts to study the more popular ruffed grouse.

"The woodcock seemed to be a neglected species. I saw the potential of the resource and how it wasn't being looked at seriously. I was also getting the Grouse Cooperator's Report started and included woodcock because I knew hunters would be getting them both.

"I don't think we had much of a population of woodcock. Hunters weren't aware of them until grouse numbers were down. "

He first used a pointing dog, a Brittany spaniel, to locate broods of woodcock for banding in the early 1960s. As of 1995, he had banded 1580 woodcock. And 1996, he says, "was the first time I did not band a single bird."

His banding and hunting efforts have taken him throughout the woodcock's range.

To Tennessee, for instance: "Even a local game warden didn't know what woodcock were. He thought they were male pileated woodpeckers and were the 'cock of the woods.'"

To South Carolina: His son reported hearing a woodcock peent and wondered if it would be a good place to hunt. "It took me about five seconds to decide to go down. I took Patch, of course." There, they enjoyed a day of 49 flushes in the Francis Marion State Forest where they hunted in the wake left by Hurricane Hugo. Deadfalls and shintangles were so thick that in order to flush the birds, one of them would have to creep up to Patch on point while the other held back to take the shot.

To Ontario: "We know that there are birds in upper Ontario and into eastern Saskatchewan. And they come from the east and across Drummond Island. We know some woodcock come across White-fish Point in fall and spring. But since there's been so little banding of birds done on the breeding grounds that far north, we just don't have the information."

And he's always ready to learn about something new or some rarely observed behavior. "Woodcock are interesting plus there's so much we don't know about them."

Andy Ammann's first name is actually George. But the "A.A." initials furnished by his nickname reveal his major passions and most cherished memories:

*A*lways the dogs. *A*lways the woodcock.

Unions and Intersections

MARCH 1997

M r. Carney, you act as if you are the king and want us all to become a bunch of princes and princesses," one high school junior complained last semester in response to my repeated suggestion that she's capable of improving her writing skills.

"No, I'd settle for your just wanting to become members of the court," I countered. "Just to want to rise above the common folk. Being unwilling to settle for mediocrity."

As they left my mouth the words sounded like a plea.

Another student asked, "What's wrong with being mediocre?"

I managed to muster a sputter, little more.

Albert Einstein said, "Knowledge is nothing without imagination." And the sobering conclusion that both confronts and confounds me is that we adults will soon give way to a new lost generation, one that lacks not the ability but the will and the need to exercise its imagination. The calculating fingers of Madison Avenue and its field marshal, television, snatch and mold children long before they reach the school yards. Didn't I read somewhere that two of the first words youngsters learn to read are *McDonald's* and *Coke*?

"You're not fair, Mr. Carney. You're so smart and you expect all of us to be, too," another student told me about a week later.

"Hold it right there!" I cautioned. "Let's get one thing straight. I'm not smart."

After a dramatic pause during which, thankfully, the following occurred to me, I continued: "All I am is curious enough to wonder about the relationships between things. You don't have to be smart to do that."

For example, I still wonder about that ruffed grouse I saw walking in fairly open woods beside an expressway in northern Michigan last month. Just wasn't where you'd expect one, since such open cover allows for quick strikes from avian predators.

We had just spent some time in Rogers City, at the tip of Michigan's mitten. There, our friend Bruce Grant regaled with this recollection: Once, while deer hunting from a tree stand, he watched a bobcat kitten climb a tree to surprise its mother, surprise itself by falling out, then fall a foot short in its attempt to jump the same creek she had. He wondered if the kitten were actually conscious of the concept of "play."

I offered the mystery which another pal and I encountered as we skied in nearby Thompson's Harbor State Park a couple years back.

"We think we found a spot where two bobcats mated," I said. "We found two sets of tracks converge onto the trail, a spot where the snow was all messed up and a few spots of blood. What do you think?"

"This is the time of the year for that," said Bruce. "That's probably what you saw."

The operative word here is *probably*.

Nature leaves behind clues and hints, rarely the entire story. Unless you hold in reserve a bounty of direct observations you can only guess at what has taken place. Like the scattered feathers I found in my backyard a couple weeks ago. I imagine a mourning dove fell prey to a hawk. Probably.

Such wildlife highlights and speculations from recent weeks won't head into the classroom with me, though. Why? I'm leery anymore of entrusting to the general population of students something as sacred and special to me as my experiences in nature. I'm weary of their belittling the notion that the majesty of nature can be found in its simplicity. I'm insulted when they react as if I'm either a geezer or a fool for trying to motivate them to consider the existence of possibilities and sensibilities other than those they exercise but rarely examine.

For example, about a month ago, to break up the tedium of explaining the directions to sophomore term papers, I asked if any of the kids had taken time to view the comet Hale-Bopp. A couple of kids started telling their stories. A few seemed interested. One kid took his usual nap.

Two weeks later his father demanded a conference.

Poor quality work had been this student's hallmark all year long, you see. He had come right out and told me that he was more interested in working 25 hours a week at a small engine repair shop than in anything I could teach him about composition and literature. The pressing problem for him at the moment was that he had submitted absolute, undeniable junk for the required research paper and had been graded as such.

His father showed up to set me straight.

During the conference I mentioned that perhaps the kid should consider if his job were taking too much of his time, for in addition to being unprepared he often slept in class.

"That's because you were talking about that planet or something and I wasn't interested and I don't have to pay attention if I'm not interested," the child sneered.

Astonished by what I had just heard, I could only look to the father for some indication of support. He merely nodded in agreement with his child.

I don't want to tell kids what I know; rather, I want to share the relationships I've discovered and nurtured:

Years ago, try 1967, I became infatuated with *Walden* after a DJ mentioned that the song "Different Drum" by Linda Ronstadt and the Stone Poneys was inspired by Thoreau. Two years ago, I found comfort in the waters of the 15th Century mystic St. John of the Cross but only because they had first been warmed by Loreena McKennitt who had set his poem "Dark Night of the Soul" to music. Last summer, I was captivated by music from *Riverdance* and one tune touched me deeply, the lament to Cuchulainn. He reappeared when I skimmed through some Irish folklore. Later, as the lament moaned on the tape player in the background, he surfaced in Thomas Cahill's, *How the Irish Saved Civilization*. Finally, in *Angela's Ashes*, using prose as rich yet as delicate as a communion wafer of shortbread to describe his childhood, Frank McCourt tells us Cuchulainn is his favorite character. Cuchulainn is the Irish equivalent of the Greek epic hero Achilles in *The Iliad*. And there on my bookshelf, waiting to be read, stands the Irish national epic, *The Tain*.

But there's more. Notice that music first set the tone for these various mental road trips. Several essays by naturalist/physician/educator Lewis Thomas in the book *The Medusa and the Snail* reveal his concept of music as the linchpin of human nature.

In a speech delivered at a medical school commencement, for example, he says, "We are a spectacular, splendid manifestation of life. We have language and can build metaphors as skillfully and precisely as ribosomes make proteins. We have affection. We have genes for usefulness. . . and finally, and perhaps best of all, we have music."

In an essay applauding a certain molecule he writes, "The capacity to blunder slightly is the real marvel of DNA. Without this special attribute, we would still be anaerobic bacteria and there would be no music."

In "On Thinking About Thinking" he writes, "Music is the effort we make to explain to ourselves how our brains work."

"Seek connections," I want to tell the students, "and you will develop insights. Ferment insight and you discover education."

You know, ol' Einstein said something else: "I have no special talents. I am only passionately curious."

I don't want my students to become princes and princesses.

I just want them to be Einsteins.

Holy Thursday

APRIL 1997

I hope by now you've done more than just take a casual glance at the comet Hale-Bopp.

Those who do so have been rewarded with their own personalized experience with the heavenly vision waltzing in the northern sky. My encounter links it to another sky dancer and to other signals a bit more subtle.

Together they are potent and mystical in their power to suggest the promise of the season.

During this, the first early spring in our new location, I've been able to witness what must be an annual resurgence of activity in the backyard. Like Maureen scurrying about in her clean-up efforts, a scattering of birds has been diving in and attacking the grasses and twigs deposited by winter. Instead of raking them into piles for recycling though, the birds snatch and recycle them into home improvement projects of their own. One mourning dove, like a choosy do-it-your-selfer at the 2 x 4 pile, selected, deliberated over and rejected three twigs for every one it carried away.

And perhaps it's because the windows at our old house had a tighter seal. More likely it's because the new house lies more in line with their flight path. But in the dark of night as we lie in bed we hear them, the Canada geese. They fly from behind us, over our shoulders following the route indicated by our northwest-pointing feet.

Like the nest-builders, they are a reminder.

Likewise the great blue heron which churns the air above a main road choked with traffic. It flutters its wings then folds them as it lands on high. To the dismay of those in a hurry behind me, I slow down taking a long enough look to confirm what my glance had suggested: a rookery, nearly a dozen nests there in the middle of the suburbs. Cool.

Though it took the sacrifice of a cottontail rabbit on the altar of pavement and potholes, a turkey vulture made a roadside appearance this week, the first I've ever seen place itself in our domestic landscape. Later that same morning, another vulture soared above the road about a half mile away in the other direction.

Above all others, one annual manifestation, the focal point of my ritual, confirms for me the arrival of spring.

At some point near the end of March the temperature will have warmed things enough to encourage me afield just before dusk. I'll head past old secret spots which are now subdivisions to my current secret spot and step from the Suburban. Relying on ears more than eyes, I'll await the call which renews each spring: the *peent* of the male woodcock as it warms up for its courtship dance.

Actually, the bird makes three distinct calls during this display. Of the three, the peent is the only one issued from the ground.

Usually, I arrive at the open field the woodcock uses as a singing ground early enough to grab a seat on its eastern edge before show time. Such a vantage offers the best viewing, for the last light of day silhouettes the woodcock once it takes flight and rises above the tree line.

This year's rendition took place last Thursday evening while, as part of their Easter worship, many other folks had headed to church to recount the story of the Last Supper and the events which followed.

My timing was off, though, and I arrived well past dusk and the overture to the first act of the evening's performance. As I quietly closed the truck's door, I heard what naturalist Aldo Leopold calls the "liquid warbling," the third of the woodcock's vocal clues, which indicated the bird was near the apex of its flight and the peak of its ardor.

Guiding my eyes with my ears, I followed its flight song and tried, unsuccessfully, to glimpse the bird while it circled the field. Then, its notes drew my eyes towards the northwest where it crossed Hale-Bopp.

My normal springtime dance date with the woodcock had commingled with the most spectacular celestial display of my life, if only for a slice of a moment. I had been blessed by the gods. What could be better?

The bird landed, settled in and began his next round of peenting. While listening, I fixed the binoculars on the comet and I considered sneaking across the field to my usual sitting spot. Then came the snort. I scanned the other side of the field until the binoculars revealed what I could not prove was a deer. Moments later, though, this horizontal blip on my lens drifted down from the edge of the field and followed its snorts into the swamp.

In his poem, *"Lacrymae Christi"* (Tears of Christ) Hart Crane talks about how "thorns freshen the year's first blood." Then:

Spill out in palm and pain
Compulsion of the year, O Nazarene ...
Lift up in lilac-emerald breath
The grail of earth again
Thy face.
From charred and riven stakes O
Dionysus, Thy
Unmangled target smile.

He addresses, without indicating a difference, both the Nazarene, Jesus of Nazareth worshipped by Christians, and the Greek god Dionysus. In their respective mythologies each suffers a tragic, bloody death and a triumphant springtime rebirth. The "unmangled target," I think, refers to the purified, reborn deity in each story. By calling it a "compulsion of the year," he's saying that somewhere deep within the collective consciousness of human nature we are bound by a common inclination. At this time of year a spiritual thirst leads each of us to identify and to drink from the spring of renewal.

For me, nothing slakes that thirst like the liquid warble of a woodcock circling a field to attract a mate.

To that libation, Hale-Bopp and the deer added a twist which will never be repeated.

For the first time in my life I sampled, undiluted, the tonic of the season: Celebration. Consecration. Communion.

I drank deeply that night.

He Talks, He Walks

JUNE 1997

U sed to be that every year just about this time my thoughts, my
passions would center on Moses. No, I'm not a tent preachin',
summertime revivalist, though the pursuit of Moses began with a
near religious experience and became nearly ritual.

The annual Moses hunt began with—

QUACK!

Pardon me as I step from the computer and through the kitchen
then down the hallway and into the guest bedroom.

"Yes, Chuckie?"

"Nothin'. I was just testing the system," my 80-year-old father-in-
law says.

"Looks like it works just fine. Now, I really don't want to sound
rude but I've got a deadline to deal with," I reply and head back to
my desk.

Charles has just had knee replacement surgery. To make things
easier on both him and his 14 children, Maureen convinced him to
convalesce at our home. When Maureen has to leave, I'm in charge.
This means we play by my rules. So I loaned him a duck call he
could use if he needs me while I'm busy doing other things.

As a matter of fact, Charles was on the trip the first time we saw
Moses. So was his son Jim and Jim's pal Web. Together the four of
us headed for Web's family cabin deep in the Upper Peninsula.

The fishing had been slow, about one hook-up for every 27.5
man-hours of angling, and those were mostly finger-length blue-
gills.

QUACK! *QUACK*!

Excuse me.

"Whaddya' need?" I call from halfway down the hall.

"I want my room to look like a duck blind."

I don't even ask. I pull a U-turn, head downstairs and retrieve a half-dozen decoys, some camouflage netting and a hunting cap. I stop in the kitchen to pour some coffee into a beat-up Thermos.

"You want me to toss a few shells and a glove into a bucket of oily water to make it more like the bottom of your boat? Maybe flatten out an ammo box to add to the mix?"

"No, this is fine. I'll quack if I need you."

"I'm sure you will."

Anyway, the monotony of not catching any fish left us yearning for something to cast a new spell. One evening as an approaching thunderstorm hastened the onslaught of darkness, Jimmer and I heard him, "*Spaloonge!*"

Web and Chuckie, yapping in the rowboat, hadn't noticed this shadow feeding on the surface of all places and moving in a counter-clockwise pattern. How unusual. Didn't know any fish did stuff like that.

We wisely kept quiet until the rain chased the other two ashore. Then I positioned the canoe and told Jim to cast about 40 feet ahead, aiming for the eleven o'clock position. His cast hit the exact spot I had indicated and—

QUACK! QUACK! QUACK!

"Now what?" I shout from my seat at the keyboard.

Seems that the Detroit Red Wings are one victory away from a four-game sweep of the Philadelphia Flyers in the Stanley Cup Finals. Seems that on the short ride home from the hospital Chuckie had seen a couple dozen cars decorated in red and white for the Wings. Brooms of various styles and sizes sprouted from other vehicles, fans encouraging the sweep of Philly. Detroit hasn't been this close to winning in 42 years and Chuckie doesn't want to be left out.

"How is that?" I ask after duct-taping a whisk broom to the crossbeam of his walker.

"I guess that's all right," he says, adjusting the red bandanna/ white handkerchief we've tied around his neck. "But someone might mistake me for a maintenance person."

"You know if you don't like it why don't you just—" I sputter while reaching to adjust the neckwear myself.

"Here, here. Don't get nasty with a sick old man."

"Anything else?"

"No."

"Then I'd like to get back to work."

So Jimmer cast toward the spot and *WHAM*!

Remember that scene in *The Natural* when lightning strikes the moment Robert Redford connects for his first major league hit? That's exactly what happened here. Simultaneously, the lure hit, the lightning flashed and from the darkness Moses stuck.

Jim missed setting the hook, so we remained, baptized in this new belief until the storm gods flashed us from the lake in no uncertain terms.

We burst in to tell—*QUACK*!—Web and Charles about our vision—*QUACK*! But they remained dry and—*QUACK*!— unconvinced, even after I revealed we had seen its dorsal fin— *QUACK*!

"WHAT?" I shout without looking up.

But the storm abated after three hours and I took Web to a bay at the other end of the lake. On my very first cast into the darkness, *WHAM*!

QUACK!

Years ago, while baby-sitting his nephew, my late buddy Danny and I didn't want to get involved in changing diapers. So the more the baby cried, the higher we turned up the volume on the TV. The thinking here—and we did not risk market testing its validity on Danny's sister-in-law—was that if we only heard the crying briefly then it must not be very important. This time, I try to employ the same stratagem on Chuckie, only with my CD player. No such luck.

"Can't you turn that down?" Charles says, shuffling through the kitchen into the office, his broom bobbing on the walker, his duck call swinging around his neck, his camouflage cap contrasting with his "Go Wings" neck attire. A hen mallard decoy follows closely behind, its anchor line tangled around the leg of the walker.

"I've been calling and calling. Two ducks even landed on the fence outside the window. But how do you expect to hear me with that *bang-bang* music turned up so loud?"

"What do you want, Charles?" I try to be polite.

"You know, I'm going to tell Maureen about this. I think I'm starting to understand why Maggie does what she does."

Maggie is our non-hunting English setter. She came to us as a stray someone had turned in to our vet. Despite the love and sleeping spots and food we've lavished on her, she attempts to escape at every opportunity. Open gate, delivery man knocking or service door to the garage left ajar, it doesn't matter. Maggie just lowers her head and trots away, like a nursing home resident who hides behind a tree during outside time and makes a break for it when everyone else has headed indoors.

"Charles, I give up," I say and push myself away from the computer. "I'm not going to get any work done. What can I do for you now?"

"Oh, nothin'. I was just sitting there and thinking about the time Jimmer and you and I went up to Web's nest. You guys found Moses. You thought it was such a big fish. Web pacing back and forth until the rain stopped, pulling on that chin hair he called a beard. You with your 'counter-clockwise feeding pattern.' I knew you were tryin' to con ol' Chuckie. Then Web's brother spoiled your whole deal when he told us there was an otter splashing around on the lake.

"Now that's a story I'd like to see you write someday."

So would I, Chuckie. So would I.

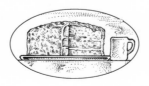

Good Afternoon

O n a typically hot day during this atypically warm autumn, the skies were high and blue, the woods were dry and the wind was holding his breath. Ambling through a ruffed grouse covert with Lucy, I was soon greeted by two realizations.

The first just kind of moseyed up and nudged me: This is the 25th season, it mentioned, that I have pursued ruffed grouse and woodcock. Twenty-five years of gaining experience, of building a bank of knowledge, of mastering my quarry.

No sooner had that notion settled into a comfortable pace with me when the second one slapped me between the shoulders and dashed away, jeering: the grouse are unimpressed.

Let me put it another way: How often do you dismiss a decent shot you make at sporting clays or during a round of skeet by saying something like, "Yeah, but on a live bird in the woods when do you ever get a chance to call 'Pull!'?"

I got mine and learned that after a quarter century of mastering my quarry, I remain an apprentice.

The parched ground cover that afternoon left little scent for Lucy's usually keen nose. As a result, her search took her and the tinkling of her bell farther and farther from me.

At one point, something—I call it "cultivated instinct"—caused me to stop and listen. From about ten yards away came the murmur of dried leaves being stirred underfoot. The feet belonged to a grouse partially hidden by a small maple. Its tail fanned from behind one side of the tree; its head popped out from the other. Its beady left eye froze me in my tracks. Its crown feathers rose to attention, a sign, all my experience has taught me, of alarm and preparation for flight.

"This is going to be so easy, " I told myself.

I adjusted my cap, glasses and gloves like some power hitter before stepping up to the plate. I even started reviewing recipes in my mind.

I shuffled forward, a half-step, then another, careful to lead with my left leg so I would continuously maintain a shooting stance, another cultivated instinct.

One more half-step and I shouted, "Hah!"

The grouse erupted from the leaf-paved runway, headed for a clearing and presented me with a wide open, going away shot. As I pulled the trigger, I envisioned the grouse tumbling to the ground.

By the time I adjusted my vision to reality, the grouse had veered left and accelerated. I fired again. I could have simply shouted again and saved the shell.

But set aside my poor shooting skills for a moment. As far as stalking the ruffed grouse goes, I had known enough to stop and listen. I had recognized that a break in the vegetation —or any variation in the cover—will often hold birds. And I had taken my time, mounting my gun and letting my ears direct my arms and eyes to the apparent, albeit inaccurate, point of intersection of the lead pellets and the bird.

Instead of playing the role of master hunter, though, I felt more like Rodney Dangerfield of the forest.

Ten minutes later, two more grouse flushed from about forty yards away, not even giving me the opportunity to confront myself once again with my poor shooting. The second flushed about ten seconds after the first. Interestingly, though, it wasn't the distinctive "whirrrrr" of their wings that had alerted me to their distant presence.

Grouse vocalizations are rare enough that two of the most popular sources for birders, the Peterson and Audubon Society field guides, focus mainly on the sounds a drumming male makes with his wings. What I heard before each bird took off was about a half-dozen, pleasant little "blurps," which sounded like bubbles popping in a lively simmering—not boiling—pot of vanilla pudding. While they did not sound like alarm or distress calls, they preceded by mere seconds the flush of the birds.

The classic study, *The Ruffed Grouse, Life History, Propagation, Management,* published in 1947 by the New York State Conservation Department refers to "the startled, 'pete-pete-pete—pete—pete' of a bird just before flushing."

I guess if the bird "petes" at a low enough tone, it might sound like pudding bubbles.

Other grouse don't offer such a warning but are just as maddening in other ways. At the moment you stomp the ground to try to flush the bird your dog is pointing, you hear two or three more taking off, not more than 20 yards away, shielded by still-green trees.

"What are you complaining about?" Maureen later asked. "As least you're hearing birds this year. Before, you used to complain that you couldn't find any."

She's got a point there. Grouse numbers are up. I just haven't been shooting that many, and not only because I'm a terrible shot.

I've actually passed up some shots, opportunities which, in years past, I would not have let slip away. I guess that's a privilege of age, finally shaking free of the urge to compete and to conquer which had lurked beside me during previous seasons in the woods and which had urged me to fire away at every bird within range.

Wildlife artist Jim Foote introduced this new outlook a couple years ago.

"Someday," he said, "you won't feel the need to shoot all the time. If you get good dog work on a wise bird, the shooting won't even matter. Then you'll be ready to enjoy the complete hunting experience, watching your dog work without feeling as if you always have to kill the bird."

In the woods that afternoon, not long after those two grouse had "blurped" their way into and out of my life, Lucy's beeper summoned: "On point!" I churned through the leaves and the sometimes tangles and found her at an edge, a deadly place for grouse to be caught.

Lucy stood tall, the last third of her tail curling back and pointing toward her head. Her body both quivered from the aroma of scent and shook from her panting. Part of her face was blocked by a young aspen; most of it bathed gloriously in sunlight. Sun and shade dappled the rest of her body.

As I stepped deeper into the scene, a longer, distorted, ebony likeness of myself inched along the ground beside me and duplicated my every move. The two of us edged closer, each leading with his left leg.

If I were an artist, this work would be entitled, "Lengthening Shadows." And the grouse crouching beneath the decaying log would be painted with crown feathers erect.

I adjusted my cap, glasses and gloves.

One more half-step and I spoke: "Happy anniversary."

No need to remain, the grouse implied with its flush, for further celebration.